Exploring World History

Ideas for Teachers

Mark Williams, Lou Ratté, and Robert K. Andrian

HEINEMANN
Portsmouth, NH

Heinemann
A division of Reed Elsevier Inc.
361 Hanover Street
Portsmouth, NH 03801–3912
www.heinemann.com

Offices and agents throughout the world

The authors and publisher wish to thank those who have generously given permission to reprint borrowed material:

Portions of Chapter 1, "World History: Not Your Ordinary Survey," originally appeared as "World History: Not Why? But What? And How?" by Robert K. Andrian in *Teaching World History: A Resource Book* edited by Heidi Roupp. Published by M. E. Sharpe, 1997. Reprinted by permission of M. E. Sharpe, Inc., Armonk, NY 10504.

Photographs on pp. 23, 117, and 118 by Wayne Dombkowski.

Library of Congress Cataloging-in-Publication Data
Williams, Mark, 1948–
    Exploring world history : ideas for teachers / Mark Williams, Lou Ratté, and Robert K. Andrian.
        p. cm.
    Includes bibliographical references.
    ISBN 0-325-00342-4 (alk. paper)
    1. World history—study and teaching (Middle school). 2. World history—study and teaching (Secondary). I. Ratté, Lou. II. Andrian, Robert K. III. Title.

D21 .W73 2001
907'.1'2—dc21   2001039344

Editor: William Varner
Production: Vicki Kasabian
Cover design: Joni Doherty
Manufacturing: Louise Richardson

Printed in the United States of America on acid-free paper
05 04 03 02 01 VP 1 2 3 4 5

To our spouses, Faith, John, and Myck,
and all our children and grandchildren from around the world

Contents

INTRODUCTION   1

PART 1

1   World History: Not Your Ordinary Survey   11
     Robert K. Andrian

2   "We're Making History": Designing
     a Curriculum for Sixth Graders   39
     Lou Ratté

3   The World After Columbus: Learning a Lot About a Little   67
     Mark Williams

PART 2

4   Beyond Eurocentrism: The View from the "Non-West"   94
     Lou Ratté

5   World History Teaching: Where Do We Go from Here?   115
     Robert K. Andrian

6   If It's Dull, It's Not History   137
     Mark Williams

EPILOGUE   163
APPENDIX: *Resources for Teaching World History*   171

Introduction

The recent development of various sets of "standards" for world history, as well as the creation of an advanced placement world history curriculum and examination, mark the arrival of a new era for the teaching of history in the schools. There was a time when world history and the history of Western civilization were not two different courses of study. In fact, before the 1980s few high school students in the United States were involved in studying the history of peoples in Africa, Asia, Latin America, or even eastern Europe. If they were, it was hardly ever in a required course, and generally in the context of "non-Western studies" that focused more on "culture" than history. Increasingly, however, teachers and curriculum leaders are revising their approaches and courses, and overall social studies curriculum frameworks and goals are reflecting a broader, more global perspective. It is for the teachers and curriculum designers of this new era that we have written *Exploring World History.*

Each one of us is a teacher, a historian, and a curriculum designer, and we have been engaged in these complementary (though often "fragmenting") enterprises for the better part of the last half century. We are excited about the way our profession is reshaping itself—and concerned too. As will become clear in the chapters that follow, we applaud the increasing dedication to world history in the schools, but, at the same time, we have observed that what often passes for world history is not substantially different or more exciting than the Western civilization courses of the past.

We have called our book *Exploring World History,* first because we hope to engage our readers in an *exploration* of new subject matter, new perspectives on more familiar subject matter, and different classroom strategies from those employed by most history teachers. Second, the word *exploring* also encapsulates a general approach that we hope teachers and curriculum leaders will adopt, both for their own continued thinking about the history of the world, and for the kinds of courses, lessons, and classroom activities they create. Finally, we will urge teachers to engage their students in explorations of the past that require creative thought and imagination.

1

In a sense, these essays relive for the reader our own explorations—that is, our experiences as we each have wrestled with the challenge of creating courses in world history. In Part 1 each of us describes a course that we designed and the objectives we had for students and for the courses as a whole. In Part 2 we reflect more broadly on the process of conceptualizing a course in world history, with special attention to pedagogical, methodological, and scholarly concerns, in ways that we hope will be of use to other teachers, curriculum planners, and scholarly consultants as they engage in the exciting work of making world history a teachable subject.

Robert Andrian begins our trio of course descriptions (Chapter 1) with "Not Your Traditional Survey," as he says. Of the three, though, this course is the most like the traditional survey in its periodization: it begins at the beginning, takes us through a classical period from 500 B.C.E. to 500 C.E., a middle period from 500 to 1500, and up to the present, concluding with a consideration of world development. What is untraditional in the course is the strong emphasis at the beginning on having students deal with issues of perspective and objectivity as those issues impinge on our understanding of the world; the use of the concept of Southernization (as contrasted to Westernization) as the organizing device for the study of the middle period from 500 to 1500; and the shift of emphasis in the last section of the course away from the usual attempt to explain European exceptionalism to the exploration of human history as the story of intercultural encounter and the changes that encounters cause.

Lou Ratté's course, focused on six cities around the world (Chapter 2), is similar to Bob's in that the linear way of organizing time into periods that used to be characteristic of European and world surveys is still present as an organizing device. The six cities do exist in time as we understand time in those periodizations: students study Hartford, Connecticut, in the twentieth century; Athens in the fifth century B.C.E.; Timbuktu in the fourteenth and fifteenth centuries during the time when it was a center of trade and Islamic learning in three West African empires; San Juan during its time as a Spanish colonial city, from 1500 to 1898; and Tokyo from the Tokugawa period beginning in 1600 through the Meiji period. The only city that exists out of time is Banaras, which, as Lou says, is treated in the curriculum as a sacred city, existing in timelessness for the pilgrims who visit it. Periodizations form the backdrop, however, to an emphasis on an array of historical concepts, such as agency, historicization, modernity, and the invention of tradition, which really serve as the undergirding of Lou's conceptualization. Her course was a collaborative endeavor involving many outside consultants (including herself) and teachers, and the mandate was to produce a world history course for sixth graders that would be non-Eurocentric. The decision for a conceptual organization scheme, drawing on a wide range of scholarly sources, was Lou's way of serving that mandate.

Mark Williams' course (Chapter 3) is in some ways the most original of the world history offerings we present here, being, as he says, about a time period shorter than the normal American history course. Mark's focus is on England and America in the period from 1492 to 1750, a period which, of course, includes Europe's discovery of the Americas and the emergence of western European states as colonial powers reaching around the world. There is an unstated equation at work here between a world coming into focus for those Europeans who were aware of all the economic, political, and cultural changes going on about them, and the world that we can glimpse 500, 400, 300 years later. Mark wants his students to see the world as his historical subjects saw it. This is clearly the world of European ascendancy, and Mark claims that it is a very good world for beginning students to engage with since, by learning a lot about a little, under Mark's tutelage, they will learn a lot about how to do history and commit to engaging in historical inquiry throughout their lives.

Implicit in our offering for consideration these three different courses is the overall point that there is no one way to teach world history. Not only are different approaches and subjects appropriate for different ages, but there are reasonable ways of developing variations even for students of the same grade level. In fact, experimentation and exploration of different approaches is essential for world history teachers in particular, for there is sharp disagreement today on what "world history" actually means. The debate about the place that Western civilization should occupy in school curricula will not soon dissipate. And where curriculum leaders have decided to strive for "balance," or "a more global perspective," or "multiculturalism," scholars and educators have only begun to talk about how students should learn about the history of non-Western societies, or about cultural change and encounters between people of different cultures, or about how such concepts as culture itself become subject to study and question when we look into the nineteenth-century origins of some of our disciplines and examine the global reach of European influence. There is, in fact, no agreed-upon "core" of knowledge that all students should know by a certain point in their schooling, regardless of efforts by the College Board to define one. Indeed, teachers, curriculum leaders, and scholars will be discussing various approaches for some time, and those who now have the responsibility to teach and design courses for young people will have to be satisfied with continuous exploration, adaptation, and revision. We teachers, historians, and curriculum designers need to be experimenting to see what sorts of approaches work really well, and to be thinking about what "work really well" means.

Part 2 of the book we address some general issues of curriculum design and classroom strategy. We all share the view that method, content, and
pedagogy are inextricably linked in the study of history: as teachers, we cannot first do one and then the other, but always have to do all three at once.
And we have all struggled to maintain the proper balance among these three
components of teaching and learning. That said, in these chapters we each
take slightly different emphases. Lou Ratté attempts to show, in Chapter 4,
how insights from contemporary study of areas outside the West have shaped
the questions she wants to raise with students. In her approach she wants to
make clear that the body of postcolonial scholarship she is most interested
in can and ought to be explored for teaching at every level of education. Bob
Andrian's Chapter 5 approaches the question of how teachers of world history, who want to engage in the voyages of exploration we have described,
ought to approach the issue of the Standards and the new Advanced Placement requirements in world history. To what degree do the Standards and the
AP course come with their own built-in method, and how can teachers best
work within those rubrics? In the final chapter, Mark Williams brings up the
matter of motivation, and talks about ways to get students "hooked on history," so that all the debate about *what* to teach will not be rendered moot,
should the *way* that teachers teach succeed in teaching nothing!

At this point some prefatory remarks regarding our various backgrounds and perspectives might help in the consideration of these essays. As
will become evident both in the discussions of the content of these particular
courses, and in our more general chapters, we all share, albeit in different
ways, a concern that as the subject of world history becomes more standardized, much of the new scholarship that has so enlivened our own teaching, as
well as our own study and research, will be bypassed. Students will lose out if
this is the direction that world history takes, but so will teachers. They will
miss the excitement of grappling with new methodologies and new stories of
the many people all around the world whose complex lives have been so
poorly represented in the past.

In order to include that great majority in the way we understand the
past, historians have needed to broaden their search for evidence and develop
new approaches to different kinds of sources that have long lain untouched in
dusty archives. In dealing with groups left out of European and American history, it is difficult, using traditional documents such as diaries, letters, and intellectual discourses, to find out much about people who could neither read
nor write. Thus, historians have moved into public records offices to look at
land and tax rolls, church registries, account books, court records, and even
jail registers. Beyond that they have "read" and analyzed works of art and music, recorded oral traditions and folklore, examined skeletons containing evi-

dence of diseases, and joined archaeologists in unearthing and studying everyday tools, utensils, clothing, and the remains of vernacular architecture.

In studying ordinary people outside Europe and America the problems the historian faces are different. Not only are there the usual problems associated with a dearth of sources, but there are at least three other issues of primary importance that teachers and scholars doing world history face. First, there is the issue of translation. Everything that comes to us as a source, whether by or about the subject we want to study, has gone through complex processes of translation, not only from one language to another, but from one culture to another, and often from one historical context to another. The longer the distance in time from the source to us, the more complicated those processes of translation have been. Second, since the late 1970s and 1980s scholars from around the world have produced a vast body of scholarship which critiques the ways in which people in the West came to understand people from other parts of the world. These scholars have been particularly interested in analyzing how colonialism influenced the ways Europeans and Americans understood the lives, histories, and cultures of those over whom they exerted political and cultural dominance. Embedded in this critical scholarship is a warning to us to at least try to avoid seeing the world as it was seen by our nineteenth-century forebears in the West. Finally, in the absence of the kinds of sources that social historians who study the West have been able to use to recover the lives of the many, colonial and postcolonial scholars have developed methodologies and approaches that appear daunting to those unaware of the theoretical apparatus being used. Much of this work is interdisciplinary, bringing together history, literary theory, anthropology, and art history and museum studies. The ramifications of this body of scholarly knowledge for world history are only beginning to be explored.

In this book, we are inviting teachers and curriculum leaders to explore some of the new subjects and methods that we have found most useful, especially those that aim at bringing to light the lives of ordinary and not so ordinary people around the world. In Mark Williams' attempt to use social history to bring students into contact with ordinary people in England and America in the 1600s, for instance, we see a perspective that needs to be investigated for societies all over the world, and that needs to be broadened to include insights from cultural studies and postcolonial studies.

When curriculum reformers first began to think about a more "global" or "multicultural" outlook, it was common to include in revised courses the study of the achievements of people such as Mansa Musa, the great emperor of Mali. The riches, art, and intellectual activity evident in his court rivaled that of any court in Europe in the Middle Ages, and, thus, the study of Mali expanded world history into Africa and challenged the perception that

Europe has always had the "most advanced" civilization. Nevertheless, the focus was still on political leaders, conquerors, and the upper crust of society. The great majority of the world's people continued to be left out. Scholars are now beginning to focus on all of those left-out people, and there is a rapidly growing body of evidence that they played a much more important, and a much more radical role in the shaping of events and ideas than has previously been understood.[1] In Chapter 5, Bob Andrian will argue for the inclusion of the Haitian Revolution in world history courses for just this reason. It is this new body of evidence, from studies of many regions and societies and viewed from the bottom up, that we are urging school teachers and curriculum leaders to explore, and to integrate into their world history courses. In Chapter 4 Lou advances the argument one step further by suggesting approaches that start with the present of various places around the world. This is one method Lou uses to bring forward the voices that have been silent or spoken for, and these voices truly do embody a multitude of perspectives on our world.

Beyond developing some awareness of what current scholarship suggests are needed revisions in our understanding of the past, teachers and curriculum leaders need to be explorers in another sense. It is our experience that curriculum designers who have actually followed the route that historians have taken, and have carefully considered the evidence and the various interpretations they have offered, are much better able to develop courses rich in both content and possibilities for serious thought. There is a variety of ways of accomplishing this type of exploration. Behind the course descriptions in Part 1 lay three different approaches to the integration of new scholarship into school curricula.

In designing his world history survey Bob Andrian worked, as chairman of his history department, with his colleagues in the department who would teach sections of the course. They had a grant to work on the course and over a period of several years attended conferences and workshops, joined history teaching networks, and read as much as they could, making very good use of the support system that has come into existence in the last decade to help teachers of world history. They knew from the beginning that they were preparing materials for ninth- and tenth-grade students and, equally, for each other. They reached consensus over how they would define history—as the story of intercultural encounter and change—and worked hard to address questions of how they could share their own excitement in collaborative work with their students.

As project scholar for an innovative social studies curriculum development collaboration in Hartford, Lou Ratté worked with consulting scholars, teachers, and several other collaborators to produce a course for young students that would be intellectually respectable, reflecting the insights of contemporary scholarship, and non-Eurocentric. In projects such as the one that produced the six cities curriculum, she suggests, several scholars are usually brought in for individual presentations without being informed about the goals of the project as a whole and the ways in which their peers are approaching their subjects. At the very least, Lou believes, there has to be collaboration among participating scholars, a process which she oversaw for her "Cities" curriculum. In the best of all possible worlds all collaborators play a part in harmonizing the intellectual, methodological, and pedagogical aspects of the curriculum.

Mark Williams, in contrast, has worked largely on his own in developing his "The World After Columbus" (Chapter 3). He began with the framework and pedagogy of a course he had taught since the late 1960s, "From Subject to Citizen."[2] The original course, a pathbreaker in social studies education, was designed to investigate Anglo-American constitutional traditions. Mark enlarged the course's horizons until the horizons became the course. Drawing on many years of research in local and social history, the inspiration of Lou Ratté's work with the Hartford project, and the eye-opening experience of a recent second round of graduate study, he explored ways that a study closely limited in chronological, cultural, and geographical scope can branch out through ever widening circles until it encompasses the known world.

All three of us have felt a renewed sense of wonder as we have explored the range of human experience that the study of the world offers. In various ways, we have been stirred by the excitement of interpretation, and we know that we teach better as a result of the wandering and wondering that we have done.

Not only do teachers need to adopt an exploratory approach in terms of their own learning about history, but also in thinking about what they should be teaching to their students. Where students and classroom activities are concerned, we advocate here an approach to the study of world history that is much like a journey of discovery—that is, we want to engage students in the same kinds of intellectual adventures we have experienced. As today's scholars strive to understand the histories of a wider range of people, so too should school teachers seek to incorporate those new understandings into their courses, even though questions regarding how to interpret those experiences will continue to divide historians. Teachers should view those divisions as opportunities to teach students the kinds of questions that historians raise, and to help them to appreciate the wide world of human experience that is opening before us as they raise these questions.

In this book we cast students as well as explorers in order to differentiate the approach of our teaching from that which sees students as receptacles into which knowledge (defined by a consensus of "authorities") is poured, mainly through the ears and eyes. Either way, students in that framework are listeners, readers (though not very critical readers), and gazers (often out the window). "Prepare them for college," said the headmaster to the exasperated young teacher in *Dead Poet's Society*. "The rest will take care of itself."

But it doesn't. Young people do not come to meaningful understandings of the world simply by listening and mimicking. They need to investigate, sort things out, think and rethink for themselves. And in doing that, they not only learn better, but they develop better learning habits, and are motivated to continue to learn about history for the rest of their lives. Good teachers have always known this, and over the past several decades, many voices have been calling for approaches to the teaching of history that involve "critical thinking," "discovery," "inquiry," "close reading" of primary sources, and the actual "doing" of history in the classroom. Some of the momentum behind the "new social studies" movement of the 1960s may have faded amidst the desire to establish "content standards" and the pressure to get students to perform better on standardized tests. Nevertheless, there can be no denying that students learn their history better when they learn to think like historians and understand how the history that most people read comes to be written. And when they share in the excitement of discovery that is fundamental to the historical discipline, they are more likely to become lifetime learners of history. At the very least, teachers could adopt an approach in which they engage in historical thinking along with their students. That is, learning history should be a joint enterprise in which both the teacher and the students explore the unknown world together.

Our goal, therefore, is to urge teachers and curriculum leaders to consider some new ways of understanding the past and to adopt creative ways of integrating these understandings into their courses and getting students excited about history, the disciplined investigation of the past. This is *not* a manual for teaching world history. Please consider it more of a collection of thoughts meant to inspire even more thought, and, perhaps, even more creative thought. It is our hope that our readers, in the process of careful, imaginative, and continuing thought, will discover exciting new ways of exploring the world that will make sense in a changing world, and will also chart out exciting ways of presenting history that will equip and inspire their students to continue all their lives to try to understand the rich complexity of the human past.

Notes

1. For a very well-written compilation of much of this research see Peter Linebaugh and Marcus Rediker, *The Many-Headed Hydra: Sailors, Slaves, Com-*
nd the Hidden History of the Revolutionary Atlantic (Boston: The Beacon
0). We were introduced to this book by Robin Kelley, who has been

participating with us in a seminar initiated by Lou Ratté in the summer of 2000 entitled "New Ways of Looking at the World: Finding Lost Voices, Shaping New Subjects." The seminar is under the aegis of the Hill Center for World Studies in Ashfield, Massachusetts, of which Lou Ratté is the director.

2. The course was created by the Educational Development Committee in Cambridge, Massachusetts, and its pedagogy was based on the ideas of Jerome Bruner. Like Lou Ratté's Hartford project, "From Subject to Citizen" and two companion courses were the product of a collaboration of pedagogical specialists, historians, and teachers who agreed to test the materials in their classrooms. A product of its time, "From Subject to Citizen" reflected the growing interest in social history in the 1960s.

1

World History
Not Your Ordinary Survey

ROBERT K. ANDRIAN

World History at Loomis Chaffee: Day One

A group of unsuspecting ninth- and tenth-grade students holds up and presents its world map drawn from memory on poster board with colorful magic markers. I am not sure how many world maps they remember from their collective pasts, but that does not matter. Other groups with their masterpieces wait patiently, listening and looking at the map presently on display. Furrowed brows seem to abound as this particular group strives to explain why North America and specifically the United States appear so large—and so central—easily dwarfing Africa and Asia combined! Another group arises and proceeds to show a map with South America somewhat oversized and with the nation of Colombia—again rather centrally located—casting a giant shadow over Brazil and Argentina. A third group's map would assuredly satisfy the natives of Greenland—and posthumously, mapmaker Mercator—and a fourth's would make the Micronesian sailor cringe as land masses appear to cover six-sevenths of the entire poster board, even though there is a fair amount of *terra incognita*. Perhaps Columbus was familiar with such a map? A general discussion ensues. "It makes sense to put your country at the center of the map," someone explains, and many agree. Thoughts of national perspective and the notion of ethnocentrism come to my mind, but the terms themselves are left unstated for the time being. "What about the size of the land masses and the bodies of water?" I inquire. "Well, you need someone reliable to get an accurate map," comes the reply. "But it depends on where the person who drew the map lives," interjects another. "Wouldn't all maps be accurate if they each had a specific function and tried to convey a certain

11

perspective?" I wondered. "Then how can we get a world map which everyone will want to use?" someone asked. "Well, you just can't do that with a flat map." "Yeah, what we need is a globe." The crowd nods in general agreement. The teacher tosses out a plastic globe. Murmurs and giggles can be heard. The student lucky enough to catch it now has to describe the location of her right index finger on the globe. The finger rests on Egypt. "It's below the Mediterranean Sea; it's bordered by the another sea on the right; it's in Africa, and it's in the Mideast," offers the student. "From the Egyptian perspective, what's the Mideast?" I ask. Saved by the bell, the class prepares to depart. "Write a short reflection on the function and power of maps," I instruct. More furrowed brows appear. "This is confusing," frets one boy. The teacher smiles. *End of Day One.*

The eminent world historian William McNeill once observed, "Try to teach world history, and you will find that it can be done."[1] The first attempt at such an enterprise in synthesis took place in 1821 at the Boston English High School where students first learned that civilization had essentially followed in the footsteps of Christianity. Later in the century the theme of progress was substituted for Providence, and the "history of the civilized world [became] the history of the Aryan, Semitic, and Hamitic races."[2] The course itself focused on political history, wars, kings, queens, popes, emperors, dates, names, the Mediterranean basin, western Europe, the New World, and briefly, Asia and Africa. As well as being a conceptual flop, it was boring.[3]

In the twentieth century, especially after World War I, world history, a required tenth-grade course—the other requirement, of course, was U.S. History—found Western Civilization masquerading as world history. Then when a "larger" world opened up to us in the 60s and 70s, thanks to the computer and communications technology and the Space Age, world history adopted a more global perspective. Unfortunately, while successful at discrediting the old Eurocentrism, the new courses fell short in creating new parameters and conceptualizations. In trying to answer the question, "What is world history?" scholars, rather than searching for key principles of selection in the midst of too much material, retreated to the safety of specialization. The results led to area studies disguised as global history.

The 1980s brought a turn inward and away from internationalism. With this historical perspective in mind, and with several conferences and institutes under our belts, the members of the Loomis Chaffee World History Planning Group began to meet in the '90s to create a one-year required course for freshmen and sophomores titled "World History." While colleague Mark Williams worked to globalize an existing course on the Anglo-American political tradition, a course that became "The World After Columbus" discussed in Chapter 3, we worked to create what we hoped would be a different kind of survey history course, one with both breadth and depth, one with a narrative, thematically based, which would allow us to periodize the world's history in ways we had not imagined before.

Above all, we wanted to ensure that this new course would begin to turn kids on to the study of world history, foster a high degree of intellectual curiosity, develop their critical and imaginative thinking skills, and cultivate other appropriate habits of the mind that we, as teachers, desire for all students of history.[4] Thus, I knew we had to avoid the death knell of any history course, that of falling prey to coverage, where more understanding turns out in reality to be less, and where little opportunity exists for students to *do* history. The goal was to have our students uncover parts of humanity's past and give meaning to them.

The challenges were obvious: to determine how most effectively and efficiently to unite the whole human past, to identify the elegant ideas that would undergird this unity, and to acknowledge that while separate peoples need separate histories and contain distinctive cultural identities, these histories and identities do not and never have existed as discrete, separate entities. Today's World Wide Web does not represent the first example of an interactive global community at work.

We decided to create a journey for our students that would allow them to compare perspectives of different peoples and cultures in a number of different historical contexts. More specifically, we wanted them to see what happened when people decide—or are forced—to move around and bump into other people. For *movement*—of people, and therefore of all they carry with them, *tangible* things like animals and plants and food and diseases and special symbols representing who they are as people, and more *intangible* things like ideas, values, customs, stories of their parents and grandparents, and so on—and *encounter*, of these tangible and intangible possessions, represent the driving forces behind world history even as we speak today as citizens of the world. Studies of cultural encounter and the changes resulting from such interaction at key junctures in world history will allow students to place their own historical and cultural identities within a larger and longer history of an ecumenical global community.

In the rest of this chapter, I would like to outline this "journey" through world history during our academic year, which consists of three terms, each about ten weeks long. But first a few thoughts about the pedagogy for this course.

Many of our young students come to history classes with pretty naive conceptions of what history is about. In a sense they have to unlearn the idea that history is simply about acquiring knowledge about the past, which is in turn a collection of right answers. In order to do this, we need to place students in the role of thinkers and historians as much as we can. They need to *do* history as much as possible so they can become comfortable with ambiguity among other things. So, a bit of chaos and confusion often exist at the start of the course as students struggle with the realization that they, not their teachers, must become the discoverers, the detectives if you will, in search of what seems to be a most elusive historical truth. Good teaching, therefore, becomes good *facilitating* as opposed to good *telling*.

Our world history staff does not use a textbook in their classes. Instead, for a number of reasons, we create our own packet of general source materials, drawn from a variety of primary and secondary sources, which we give to the students at the beginning of each of the three terms. While it is true that more recent attempts at textbook writing do come closer to our conceptualization of what an effective one-year world history survey can be, the staff believes that textbooks too often lure teachers into *covering* history and becoming beholden to their syllabi. Students do not get to do history as much; they are not as successful at cultivating key habits of the mind like critical thinking skills, and therefore they tend to accept the words of textbook authors, usually a group of distinguished scholars, as gospel. They also tend to lose motivation about the reading itself. What about the forthcoming Advanced Placement World History, a one-year course designed for tenth graders, with the first AP Test to be administered in May 2002? Can such a course be taught without a textbook? More on this subject in Chapter 5 where we take a closer look at the AP course and what it is we think students should really know and understand.

Another pedagogical consideration has to do with the interrelationship between teaching and assessment. You will notice below as the course unfolds that each teaching unit begins with key questions, which the teacher wants the students to wrestle with, followed by the assessments, which will provide teachers with the evidence they need to measure their students' understanding. This organizational approach stresses the important premise that assessment is a vital part of teaching and learning, *not* what we as teachers do when teaching is over. Thus effective curriculum design begins with goals and essential focus questions followed by a variety of assessments used to measure student achievement of the different targeted goals.[5] Only after completing this process should teachers begin to plan day-to-day learning activities; too often teachers tend to work in reverse at the cost of validity and reliability when they finally sit down to make up the test. Moreover, the world history staff at Loomis Chaffee, like many teachers across the country, believe that if in-depth student understanding is to be evaluated, then performance tasks and projects—where the task, the criteria, and the standards are known in advance by the students and guide their work—must be given. These *authentic* assessments differ from more traditional quizzes and tests and essays in that they allow students to use their knowledge in contexts similar to ways in which adults would have to use their knowledge. The tasks themselves, examples of which are described in more detail below, require students to address an identified *real world* audience, and they tend to be more engaging and motivating to students.[6]

Finally, in this world history survey course, much of the students' work is done collaboratively. As teachers we believe that everyone does not have to study the same things all the time. We also subscribe to the idea that students can teach other students in powerful ways. When students in your class take notes on what their peers are saying rather than wait for you the teacher to go to the board to deliver the *truth*—namely, what might appear on the next test—that is a hopeful sign. To be sure, working effectively in small groups takes lots of practice. For young teenagers, the challenges of managing people and the flow of ideas and of delegating responsibilities in group settings are immense. And yet, over the course of the school year, group presentations tend to become more sophisticated, more elaborate, more theatrical, more technologically advanced. As you read about the course, you will discover a number of these group-oriented learning activities. So let's get right to it.

Term 1: Perspectives, Beginnings, Empire and Civilization, Cultural Diffusion

Introduction: Thinking About Perspective and History

Key Questions

- What is geographical perspective and why is it important?
- What do we mean by culture, cultural perspective, and cultural identity?
- What do we mean by history? Why is history important to people?

Assessments

- Daily, informal, journal-like writing where students "reflect" on what they have read and discussed.
- Diagnostic analytical essay on perspective—for example, the function and power of maps—or on cultural identity and encounter—for example, the Lost Colony of Roanoak.

Cultivating both geographic and cultural perspective in students' minds will help them to develop a degree of cultural empathy as well as to deepen their understanding of cultural encounter and change in various historical contexts. Attempts at encouraging this kind of thinking begin with *Day One* as described above. In wrestling, as students certainly did that first night, with the notion of the function and power of maps, and in examining various kinds of map projections, students begin to wonder about the intent of mapmakers, what historical and cultural factors prompted their cartography, and what uses their maps have been put to over time.[7] Students come to realize that every flat map is subjective in that it cannot help distorting the sizes and shapes of the earth's features. In the end, that such maps are bedeviled by an inherent contradiction; namely, "a claim to represent objectively a world they can only subjectively present, a claim made to win acceptance for a view of the world whose utility lies precisely in its partiality," reflects the political and cultural ramifications of geographic perspective.[8] Our own cultural conditioning, which breeds a healthy dose of ethnocentrism, can sometimes lead us to believe that *our* way is *the* way. Unhealthy ethnocentrism or chauvinism or exceptionalism is quickly reflected in the cultural stereotyping and cultural lumping of other peoples, a practice that contradicts the reality that humankind throughout world history has devised *different* solutions to common problems such as survival, order, and development. An anthropological piece, entitled "Body Ritual Among the Nacirema"—Nacirema is American spelled backward—functions as an effective source in raising student awareness about these issues. Thus early in the world history course, students are confronted with the significance of cultural perspective.[9]

Some of the teachers who staff the world history survey choose to highlight this significance by presenting to the students a case of cultural encounter. Students in the role of historians in group presentations and individual essays attempt to ascertain why the late sixteenth-century English colony of Roanoak disappeared. Among other questions, students have to address to what extent cultural contact between English migrants and Algonquins was responsible for what happened. What do they do about the fact that no sources from the natives exist to be read? What does that fact suggest about the study of history?

In this introduction to the notion of perspective and the concept of history, we expose students to the idea of *Big Geography*. Is it conceivable, for example, not to view the arbitrary designation of the continents of Africa, Asia, and Europe as three distinct land masses, but to see them as one solid land mass called *Afrasia*? Afrasia contains a Great Arid Zone that includes the west end of the Sahara, the Arabian desert, which the Red Sea breaks, and then China and the Gobi Desert. In this conception the contribution of the unsettled or nomadic peoples who inhabit this arid zone to the dynamics of world trade may be recognized. One might also envision the Mediterranean Sea as a big lake and the Red Sea as a small one. And, by viewing Europe, Africa, and Asia on a geographic continuum, the *Age of Exploration*, for example, can be seen in its proper world-historical context. Thus, "Portugal and Spain do not magically initiate exploration and trade, but act within an already existent, often dynamic system of world exploration and trade and communication [begun long ago]."[10] Similarly, Big Geography affects our labeling of oceans. Why not picture the Indian and Pacific Oceans as one enormous body of water, which would help to explain how the peoples of the Southern and Eastern Hemispheres assisted in connecting the world for so long before Prince Henry the Navigator and Christopher Columbus. Such a view gives students more accurate historical context, but has the added advantage of recognizing the perspective and predominance of *water*, while the usual perspective of land—many maps in Columbus' day had land covering six-sevenths of the earth's surface—takes a back seat.

In the final portion of the course introduction, students think about the role and power of myth by comparing various creation myths from different cultures. People remember the past as a means to give meaning to their lives and in effect use their histories to create, sustain, and develop their cultural identities and their cultural traditions. Here we consider the significance of religion in creating order out of chaos in societies. Introducing students to creation myths early in the course offers additional advantages. The stories of peoples' origins can also give students different conceptions of time—for example, linear versus cyclical time—and even space, affording the teacher an opportunity to return to compare and contrast these cultural conceptions as the course evolves. And myths, because they raise and answer several questions related to the concept of religion—the relationship of man to the Creator, the means to form order from chaos, the question of life after death, to name a few—can begin to help students formulate a working definition of religion, which will be essential as they investigate the spread of universal religions later in the first term. Many of these myths illustrate a "Mother Earth–Father Sky" paradigm, which will be useful in discussing gender relations and issues of power, and which invariably prompts a few students to wonder how and why the paradigm begins to change as the agricultural revolution gives way to its urban counterpart. Fittingly then, the introduction to world history concludes with a selection from *The Epic of Gilgamesh*, which allows students, through myth, to explore changing gender roles and status, conceptions of what is *civilized* and what is *primitive*, and relationships between the *urban* life and the *hinterland* or *wilds* or pastoral or nomadic life.[11]

Investigation No. 1: Classical Civilizations: A Comparative Study

Key Questions

- During the Classical period—500 B.C.E.–500 C.E.—what enduring cultural characteristics developed in these civilizations which would later influence other cultures when they encountered them?
- What did it mean to be Greek, Chinese, Indian, Roman?
- What might happen if these societies encountered each other?

Assessments

Group: Design a wing of a museum dedicated to your civilization.

Individual: At a dinner party, create a dialogue among invited guests from the four civilizations that would illustrate what would happen when they encountered each other. The students must choose three major topics of discussion. Some of the topics might include the existence of equality, order, gender relations, government, family values, the individual, and the state.

As a prelude to their first group investigation, students first design their own ancient cities. Then the entire class looks at Israel as a model of a civilization and brainstorms what exhibits to include in a "model" museum wing dedicated to ancient Israel. The class then divides into four groups, each responsible for working with a packet of sources, mostly written but some visual, which the teaching staff has assembled to investigate each of the civilizations chosen.[12] As much as possible we would like these source materials to be primary in nature with secondary sources providing necessary historical context and, at times, interpretation. Much of the original source material comes from the primary source readers listed in the appendix. Our world history staff has created a number of historical background essays. Members of the group divide up readings and come to class each day for three days to discuss what they have read. Learning to work effectively with primary sources is an important part of this first investigation, along with, of course, learning to work together as people; thus each student must keep a well-organized notebook and must follow guidelines for working with sources as the historian would. Each group must determine the hallmarks of each civilization, and the source packets are geared to helping them do so. Each of the packets focuses on the concept of cultural identity, and each includes materials that address gender issues. The groups must then plan a museum exhibition illustrating their respective cultural identities. When all the groups have presented their exhibitions, and general discussion has concluded, then students must put together their dialogues individually.

Transition to Investigation No. 2

Part of this interlude between group investigations involves both students and teacher assessing how the group presentations went and how they can become more effective. The entire class then looks at the description of four cosmopolitan cities each situated within empires that fostered cross-cultural contact during the period from 500–1500 C.E. Reading descriptions of Chang-an, Constantinople, Baghdad, and Timbuktu, students raise questions centering on all the long-distance trade that was taking place and the multicultural composition of urban life in these cities. These questions help to serve as guidelines for the upcoming investigation into global interconnection through cultural interaction.

Another transitional approach might have students engage in a simulation activity designed to illustrate how networks of trade in the Indian Ocean fostered the exchange of commodities, notably spices, and the spread of technology, disease, and religion.[13] As additional background to the investigation, students begin to pursue some of the questions just raised by first examining the cross-cultural spread of a disease, the fourteenth-century Bubonic Plague. The entire class considers the comparative regional impact of the pandemic known as the Black Death. Making comparisons with origin, migration, and impact of HIV-AIDS can be enlightening for the students. Finally, all students explore the concept of *Southernization*. In part, especially concerning the role of trade in spreading both goods and ideas, especially sacred ideas, they learn that the North and the West must wait a long time before catching up with a richer and more prosperous South and East. The list is rather impressive from these southern and eastern regions of the globe:

- Indian cotton and mathematics — our numerals including the number zero may have been delivered by the Arabs, but they are indeed from India
- Molucca Island spices — cloves, nutmeg, cinnamon, pepper
- Chinese silk, porcelain, gunpowder, and, of course, the compass
- Arab traders and Muslim pilgrims and travelers across the Sahara and throughout Asia
- Mongol conquests of Muslim areas opening up trade routes between Mediterranean Europe and the Pacific

- Marco Polo and the appearance of printing, the compass, and gun-powder in Italy
- A Turkish-Mongolian-Iranian Muslim cultural mix expanding into eastern Europe, Southeast Asia, and East and West Africa

And all of this activity *before* the Columbian exchange![14] Doing map work with the students to illustrate the process of Southernization makes great sense at this juncture.

In addition to commercial activity, Buddhism migrated along the Silk Road from India to China and then found its way to Southeast Asia. Another of the world's great universal religions, Islam, spread rapidly into various parts of Central and West Asia, Southeast Asia, Africa, and southern Spain. And Christianity made its way throughout the Roman Empire. As a final piece of preparation for their second investigation, students read about the rise and spread of Christianity in western and eastern Europe and the Levant.

Investigation No. 2: The Interactive Global Community

Key Questions

- What was the state of the world like in the mid-fifteenth-century?
- What factors were responsible for so much of the world becoming linked together?
- What was the impact of all of this cultural contact on various peoples and societies?

Assessments

Group: Each group needs to plan an engaging presentation—maps need to be included—that helps the rest of the class to understand how the world got to be the way it was by the mid-fifteenth-century.

Individual: Borrowing from Mark Williams' similar assessment in his course, "The World After Columbus"—see Chapter 3—students have to critique a phony excerpt from a textbook, created by the teacher. The excerpt, written by the fictitious Professor H. Liam Aeroprone— "I Am Errorprone" in translation—for the managing editor at the similarly fictitious publishing company, Truth Unlimited, Inc., pro-fesses to be the truth about the state of the world in the early fifteenth century and how it got to be that way.

Once again packets of materials are distributed to four groups. I like to keep the composition of the groups the same as the first time so that they may work

Figure 1–1. *A group presentation on the Mongol empire's impact*

together again to improve on the areas in need. For this investigation, the four groups are:

1. the rise and spread of Islam with special focus on West Africa
2. the Silk Road trade and the spread of religion into China and Southeast Asia
3. the impact of the Mongol conquests with focus on Marco Polo
4. travelers and adventurers by land and by sea: Ibn Battuta, Prince Henry the Navigator, and Zheng He

Engaging primary sources can be difficult to find for these groups, though new materials coming out are encouraging.[15] The challenge to the teacher, of course, is to remain ever the facilitator. A successful student group often can carry on its discussion while the teacher sits in rather than quickly making the teacher the focus of the conversation. Successful presentations can take on many forms combining the written and the visual, but teachers need to make the criteria for evaluation clear and disseminate it ahead of time (see Figure 1–1). After the presentations and general discussion, students work on and submit the first draft of their critiques, the final draft to be turned in just prior to the winter holiday break in mid-December.

In lieu of the traditional kind of final exam for the fall term, students submit their notebooks. Obviously the contents and organization of the notebook are very important, but we want them to go further in their thinking about what they have learned and how they have learned it during these first ten weeks of the year. Thus, each notebook must have a title page which, in the mind of each student, captures the meaning of the fall term. An introductory page follows, which essentially defends the choice of the title. Students also spend time evaluating their own performance in the class thus far by answering such questions as: what changes do I need to make next term in order to narrow the gap between what I intended to do and what actually happened?

Term 2: Connecting the Rest of the Globe: From *Southernization* to *Westernization*

Cultural Encounter in the Cosmopolitan World of Arab/Islamic Spain, 711–1492

Key Questions

- In what ways did the cultural milieu of al-Andalus, Muslim Spain, encourage cultural diffusion?
- What impact did the Christian Reconquest of Spain have on this milieu?
- What legacies were left by al-Andalusian civilization and Islamic science in general?

Individual Assessment

Write a revision of Professor Aeroprone's text for the Managing Editor at Truth Unlimited, Inc., publishers of history textbooks all over the world.

The quirks of our academic calendar have us returning from one school vacation, Thanksgiving, only to embark on another, Christmas for most students, only three weeks later. In actuality the block of time—about ten to twelve classes in all—fits our needs perfectly. We wanted to have the interactive global community come alive for our students by having them explore the cultural impact of Arab/Islamic civilization in southern Spain or al-Andalus. Audrey Shabbas, founder of AWAIR, Arab World and Islamic Resources and School Services, has developed a wonderful learning activity titled the *A Medieval Banquet in the Alhambra* where students role-play various personalities, literary, artistic, philosophical, religious, royal—many alive in tenth- and eleventh-century Granada, some brought ahead from the dead, some brought back from the future—from all over the Islamic world and beyond. Throw in authentic Arabian cuisine, prepared by our dining hall, homemade costumes, music and dance, poetry recitation, the performance of

Figure 1–2. *Alhambra Banquet guests sample the authentic Arabian food*
Photo by Wayne Dombkowski

a play, and the interruption of the banquet by the Spanish Inquisition, and you have all the makings of an extravaganza that functions as a highly effective learning experience (see Figure 1–2).[16] Listening to St. Thomas Aquinas acknowledge the reality that the Islamic thinker Ibn Rushd influenced his thinking that faith and reason could be compatible allows students to consider the role Arab/Islamic civilization played in preserving, elaborating, and passing on Greek and Indian science and mathematics. Hearing the Chinese inventor Pi Sheng talk about printing with Johan Gutenberg next to him on the stage permits students to contextualize the growth of technology and the European Renaissance in broader, world-historical terms. When Ferdinand and Isabella—and Columbus in the background—simulate the conquest of Granada in 1492 by putting an end to the Arabian play being performed, by collecting infidel books and burning them, and by expelling Jews and Muslims from the banquet hall, students experience firsthand some of the significance of the Christian Reconquest.

As students rewrite their critiques, they watch the film *The Name of the Rose*, based on the novel of the same title by Umberto Eco, which explores the relationship between the love of God, the love of knowledge, and the love of humanity. Set in a Benedictine monastery in fourteenth-century Italy, the film helps students compare and contrast the Islamic and Christian positions on faith and reason.

Global Interdependence: The Columbian Exchange and Factors Affecting European Exploration and Expansion

Key Questions

- What was the significance of Columbus' voyages in terms of ongoing transhemispheric systems of trade and cultural contact?
- What factors, external and internal to Europe, explain Europeans' success at discovering the Americas and circumnavigating the globe, as opposed to Chinese or Arabs'?

Individual Assessment

Ongoing reflective writing in students' journals contained in their notebooks

When the students return from the winter holiday vacation, they do confront Columbus, who sailed the ocean blue, but learn to contextualize his "Enterprise of the Indies" not as a stage in the evolution of European history—what one would find in a traditional Western Civilization course—but as part of larger patterns in long-distance exploration and trade and cultural contact. Hence students focus both on the initial perceptions of the Tainos and Spanish on their encounter and on the incredible hemispheric exchange of plants, animals, and diseases that followed. Looking at the travels of the Andean potato and the Iberian horse and the diseases of smallpox and syphilis, for example, can prove very effective in getting students to think more deeply about the cultural impact of the Columbian voyages. As a continuing introduction to the first group investigation of this second academic term, students read a staff-composed essay that highlights motivations for European exploration and the lack of necessity for Chinese or Arab exploration westward. Some external factors, such as the lure of spices, wealth, and potential converts to Roman Catholicism, and the threat of a resurgent Islam in the form of the Ottoman Turks, *pulled* Europeans across the Atlantic. Other internal factors, such as the Renaissance, the Protestant Reformation, and Catholic Counter-Reformation, and the emergence of powerful nation-states—Portugal, Spain, England, France, and the Netherlands—and their competition for trade and possessions around the globe, *pushed* Europeans across the ocean. Such historical context will serve students well as they move next to investigate cultural encounters in the Americas and Asia in the sixteenth and seventeenth centuries.

Investigation No. 1: Encounters in the Americas and Asia

- Mexico: Spanish and Aztecs
- Peru: Spanish and Incas
- Canada: French and Canadian Indians
- New England/Connecticut: English and Pequots
- Japan: Portuguese and Japanese
- Indonesia: Dutch and Natives

Key Questions

- Why does the cultural encounter between Europeans and natives lead to so much violence and such a tragic ending for the indigenous peoples?
- Why does the outcome of the Japanese and Portuguese encounter seem to be so different in terms of the changes it wrought?

Assessments

Group: Make a presentation based on a packet of materials prepared by the teacher.[17]

Individual: Write an analytical essay that addresses the key questions noted above. The essay could also be written in the form of a historical—nonfictional—narrative, though in either case, the teacher must be sure students have rubrics for each style.

Once again, as with previous group presentations, they may take on different forms. Some might prefer to focus on the visual and offer a display of some kind; others might prefer to "perform" live with skits or role plays; others may opt for submitting detailed written outlines; others by putting together a video; and still others, depending on their facility with technology, working with Power Point or Hyperstudio. Regardless of the choice, teachers need to be diligent in helping students negotiate the challenges of perspective and point of view present in the sources they are provided with in their packets and in the sources that are glaringly and annoyingly absent. What can we learn about the cultural and historical context each group finds itself in? What should the historian do, for example, when there are no eyewitness accounts from the Connecticut Pequots in their devastating 1636 war with the English? What about the Aztec accounts of their demise as seen through the lenses of Spanish missionaries who put the natives' reminiscences on paper? What can we make of Bartolome Las Casas, for example, the Spanish missionary who condemns the savagery of the conquistadores but who also sees Christianity as the means to civilize the natives? How should we evaluate the validity of the film *Black Robe*, based on a novel, which offers a compelling interpretation of the encounter between French Jesuits and the Algonquins, not to mention the encounters between Algonquins and Iroquois? What do we do with all of the "lost voices"? Is the oral history of Native Americans really not history? As a staff, we world history teachers spend a good deal of time addressing questions like these. We also let each individual teacher choose three of the cultural encounters listed above along with the Portuguese-Japanese encounter.

Beginning this group investigation by having everyone watch *Black Robe* serves as an effective introduction to these cultural encounters and elicits a number of thoughtful questions from the students, which help to frame their analysis. For our purposes, ending this unit by taking all of the students to the Mashantucket Pequot museum, in Ledyard, Connecticut, allows the students to see firsthand a re-creation of Pequot history and culture and think about the Pequot interpretation of the cultural conflict between the English and their forebears.

Transition to Investigation No. 2

During the second group investigation students will examine a number of case studies focusing on the impact of the eighteenth-century Atlantic slave trade in various regions of the Americas. Before that, however, we want to introduce them to slavery and the slave trade in West Africa. One way to do this would have the students read excerpts from the narrative of Olaudah Equiano, also known as Gustavus Vassa, a West African boy uprooted from his family along with his sister, stuffed into a slave ship, and sold into slavery. While not typical in terms of his lifetime experiences—Equiano earned his manumission and became a critic of slavery—his story elicits a number of thoughtful questions from students about the institution of slavery and the complexities of the slave trade from both an African and European perspective.[18] Additional readings, for example, a letter in 1526 from the Kongolese king, Nzinga Mbemba, whose Christian name was Afonso, to the Portuguese King Joao III, bemoaning some of the effects of the slave trade yet not calling for its complete abolition,[19] begin to attempt to answer some of these questions, and begin to place the slave trade in larger world-historical contexts. Students role-play an early eighteenth-century gathering of Africans and Europeans meeting to discuss issues surrounding the slave trade in the Dahomey kingdom, led by King Agaja.[20] They become aware of the conflicting views among both Africans and Europeans—a British missionary, for example, condemns the evils of the slave trade while maintaining that the Africans cannot include themselves in the civilized peoples of the world, namely the Europeans—and of the vicious political and economic cycle created by the slave trade. Conditions around the entire Atlantic combine to encourage the involuntary migration of millions of Africans to the Americas. An analysis of the slave trade requires understanding commercial rivalries among competing mercantilist European nation-states and struggles for power among various West African ethnic groups in the wake of the demise of the Songhay empire. In addition African migrants could withstand various diseases while Native American populations could not, making the former group logical choices to be enslaved. Students write reflectively after the role play in an effort to analyze and synthesize what they have learned.

Investigation No. 2: Atlantic Slave Trade Encounters in the Americas

- North America: Chesapeake, Carolina, and Georgia Sea Islands
- North America: New York
- Caribbean: Haiti
- South America: Brazil

Key Questions

- How were the identities of African slaves and their descendants affected by their experiences as slaves?
- What sorts of responses did Africans make to the situations in which they found themselves? Were they able to affect their livelihoods in any ways?
- What relationship existed between slavery and racism?

Assessments

Group: Put together a group narrative that tells the story of the encounter between African slaves and their colonial masters using the key questions as guidelines.

Individual: Write an individual narrative that synthesizes the four group narratives, or write an analytical essay that addresses the question, what was the significance of the Atlantic slave trade?

The students will not be performing for their presentations this time. Instead they will work together to compile a "story" and their interpretation of that story based on the guideline questions noted above, using their packets of materials.[21] In this case, some of the sources will be visual and aural including video clips of music and dance from the various regions being studied.[22] While the sources depict the often horrific nature of slave life under the domination of European slave masters, they also help students to understand that Africans were not simply passive victims but were able to find various means of resistance and rebellion. In the case of Haiti, such rebellion meant an outright, successful revolution, one which we will consider more carefully in Chapter 5. These materials also illustrate the practices of cultural diffusion and syncretism and their impact upon African and European identities. Georgia Sea Island songs, for example, combine African rhythms and the use of drums and call-and-response singing with strong references to the Old Testament. (The compact disc is listed in the appendix.) Of course, use of Christianity did not necessarily mean acceptance, as adherents of the African religion of vodoun would demonstrate in Haiti.[23] On the other hand, a tradition of Christianity in the Kongo may have played a part in the Stono Rebellion in South Carolina.[24] Historians and anthropologists disagree over how much African culture remained intact in different regions during slavery.

After each student has read all four group narratives, a general discussion ensues that looks for points of comparison and contrast amidst change and continuity brought on by these encounters. A feature film, *Sankofa*—all films are listed in the appendix—follows and, while not for the fainthearted, it examines powerfully the impact of the slave trade on African identity. The word *sankofa* means that in order to look forward, one has to look back to traditional foundations of one's cultural identity, something akin to Alex Haley's *Roots,* if you will. Discussion of the film helps students crystallize their ideas, and they go on to generate either a narrative or analytical essay as the final assessment of the second term.

Term 3: Challenges to Authority and Identity

- Revolution
- Nationalism and Imperialism/Colonialism
- World War and Independence
- Development

Challenges to Authority: Revolutions in the Seventeenth, Eighteenth, and Nineteenth Centuries

Key Questions

- What kinds of challenges to attempts at maintaining absolute authority occurred during this time?
- How much change was actually brought about by these revolutions?
- To what extent did the rights of individuals and groups change?

Assessment

Individual: Create a two- to three-page reflective piece titled: "Challenges to Absolute Authority"

The rise of the West and the process of Westernization gain significant momentum with the advent of the Industrial Revolution, built on the backs of slave laborers in the eighteenth century and the acceleration of political and economic nationalism and subsequently imperialism and colonialism in the nineteenth century. And yet, challenges emerged to the authority of religious dogma and political absolutism, first in the form of the European Scientific Revolution and Enlightenment. In the late eighteenth and nineteenth centuries, resistance and rebellion and revolution occur both in Europe and the Americas. Later, in the nineteenth and twentieth centuries, challenges to primarily European, but also American and Japanese attempts at colonial domination in the twentieth century occur around the globe. As a result of these confrontations, the identities of individuals and of nation-states and of empires underwent significant changes. Revolutionary ideals themselves, such as freedom and equality and justice, were not limitless, as slaves, women, unsettled and indigenous peoples, and those from social classes outside power structures often discovered.

We begin this final term by having students simulate a French Enlightenment salon replete with Quantz and Gluck in the background, makeshift costumes, and roles for the students to play. In a sense we want this gathering to be a discussion among, mostly but not exclusively, Europe's great thinkers. Two main issues provide the focus of the discussion: which serves man better, faith or reason, and what is Man, and what, if any, are his rights? Invited guests include European scientists and thinkers—revolutionaries like Copernicus and Galileo and Newton and Vesalius and Harvey, along with female scientists such as Maria Sibylla Merian and Emilie du Chatelet, religious figures like the Pope and Cardinal Bellarmine, who threw Galileo in jail, Chinese and African and Islamic professionals who have contributed to the *evolution* of scientific and intellectual advancement, kings like Louis XIV and Peter the Great, philosophers like Voltaire and Rousseau and Locke—yes, Jefferson is there, too—and advocates of women's rights such as Olympe de Gouges and Mary Wollstonecraft. Processing the two-day salon can lead students to consider the concepts of absolutism and constitutionalism and the relationship between science and democracy as well as to recognize the complex nature of the personalities involved. For example, Voltaire, while a proponent of religious toleration and a critic of royal officials' censorship, had no objection to slavery, did not support the Haitian revolution, and had a hard time seeing Africans as "Men." Male scientific revolutionaries had no time for their female counterparts. Some, like William Harvey, who discovered the circulation of blood, propagated theories that helped to "confirm" the innate inferiority of woman and her reproductive role.

Students then go on to do some readings about European political absolutism, the struggle among European nation-states for empire resting on the policy of mercantilism, and constitutionalism focusing on John Locke and the England's Glorious Revolution. They then read a staff-composed essay that examines the American and French Revolutions and subsequent Latin American revolutions. A literary selection from Cuban novelist Alejo Carpentier's *Explosion in a Cathedral* allows the students to look more closely at the Haitian Revolution, its incredible significance as the only successful slave revolution in world history, and its exposition of the hypocrisy of French Revolutionary ideals. At the end of the unit, students write a reflection entitled, "Challenges to Absolute Authority," where they attempt to analyze and synthesize what we have done to that point.

Investigation No. 1: Encounters Resulting from European Cultural Imperialism

- China
- Vietnam
- West Africa
- India

Key Questions

- What were the consequences of European and any other nation's intervention in other peoples' lives?
- How did these different peoples respond to such intervention? Were there different responses within the same societies?
- How were peoples' identities affected?

Assessments

Group: Each group creates a display—consisting of maps, meaningful illustrations, captions, quotations from primary sources with explanations—that illustrates what was happening in their region of the world in the nineteenth and early twentieth centuries. The difference in this investigation is that the students must find the source materials on their own in the library and then put together a display.

Individual: Write an analytical essay that addresses the three questions listed above. Evidence is to be gathered from the four group displays and from general discussion.

As an introduction to this investigation, students watch a video about the origins of the Industrial Revolution in England and its impact on imperialism and colonialism. Then we look at the response of three different societies, the Ottoman Empire, the Russian Empire, and the Tokugawa Shogunate in Japan, caught in the throes of Westernization. Only in the last case is the European challenge, if that is the right word, met. How effectively it is met, however, is another matter. "Catching up with the West" suggests that modernization meant Westernization to the Meiji rulers, and that such "progress" would be equally beneficial for all concerned in the society. Such a proposition is highly debatable. Finally students read excerpts from Kipling's *The White Man's Burden,* an effective way to begin to explore the European colonialist mind-set.[25]

As noted above, the students are responsible for finding their sources in this investigation. We, their teachers, along with our reference librarians, help them in this endeavor, but we want to see to what extent they can think along the lines of the historian, in this case, the world historian. By this time in the year, we hope their thinking skills are stronger, and that they have begun to understand more about the study of history. They know they will need background material about their region's encounter with the Europeans, so we must work with them concerning the best available historiography—we try to avoid encyclopedia and textbook sources—and they know they will need to hear from the native voices as much as possible, paying attention to perspective, point of view, audience, context, and so forth. The task is a challenging one, and that is why we wait until the final term before doing it. Generally, though, the students confirm our suspicions that they are maturer at exploring the dynamics of cultural encounter.

I have found it helpful, where possible with group presentations, to offer models to the students beforehand. In this investigation, I focus on Japanese imperialism and colonialism in East Asia and put together a display board reflecting my responses to the three key questions for the unit. Student displays invariably outdo me from the standpoint of aesthetics, and at least they have a good idea of what is expected of them substantively. Another model display might address American imperialism in Hawaii and the Philippines.

Transition to Investigation No. 2

Our next group investigation will focus on anticolonial movements for national independence, but in order to get there, we first try to establish a context for these movements by looking at the two World Wars and what I call *humanity's inhumanity*, the rise of totalitarianism, and more specifically, Hitler and the Holocaust, Stalin and his purges, and Japanese brutality in China. We also consider the dropping of the atomic bomb and the rise of the Cold War. Readings come from primary sources—some visual—for the most part, especially the war experience and the experiences of those under Nazism and Stalinism and Japanese fascism, though we use secondary material to help the students understand the global nature of the world wars, and in particular, how they helped to fuel anticolonial sentiment among various populations around the globe.[26] At the conclusion of this transitional work, students submit a reflection trying to make some sense of the first half of the twentieth century. We are not looking for in-depth analysis here. We want students to try to give meaning to this period of time and to finish the reflection by raising a number of questions in their minds that remained unanswered.

Investigation No. 2: Anticolonial Movements for National Independence

- India
- Africa
- Vietnam
- Palestine

Key Questions

- What factors helped the colonized achieve their independence?
- Was there a consensus among indigenous peoples?
- How were the identities of peoples and societies affected by these movements?
- What comparisons and contrasts were you able to discover? How do you explain them?

Assessments

Group: Given a packet of source materials,[27] create a presentation—the choice of what kind is yours—that addresses how your nation or society was able to break loose from the yoke of colonialism.

Individual: Create a narrative essay that uses the key questions as guidelines. Essentially what is the story of anticolonialism really about?

We know that the twentieth century has not only been a century of war, but one also marked by the demands of indigenous peoples in the colonized regions of the world to secure the right of self-determination in the face of resistance from Western *democratic* nations who fought world wars to preserve democratic ideals for themselves, but who also wanted to maintain control of their nineteenth-century possessions. We want students to explain and interpret these independence movements by examining them in light of their respective society's goals and ambitions, and various perspectives within those societies. A number of questions come to mind that we hope some of our students will raise and wrestle with, among others. Why did not a unified India emerge? Can we learn anything about the complexities of cultural identity and how it can change from the formation of the state of Bangladesh from East Pakistan? What role did Vietnamese history play in their success in evicting the French? What about those Vietnamese whose identities were heavily influenced by French culture? Why did nonviolence not work in Kenya? Was there a better way to settle the question of Palestine? Is there today? What role did identity play in bringing about liberation? Did the outcome change what mattered most to people in these societies?

After general discussion of each group's interpretations, students begin to write their essays while watching the feature film *Gandhi*. While containing its share of historical inaccuracies—Gandhi, for example, was never beaten by the police in South Africa—and while minimizing the important role played by the Muslim leader Jinnah in the quest for an India free of British rule, *Gandhi* is a beautiful film, powerful and entertaining, a film which, despite its length, the students enjoy watching.

Final Project: Development and Identity

Invariably upon completion of the previous unit, a student will ask about what has happened to these nations since they broke free from European domination or attempts at hegemony. "How are they doing today?" students will query. The students have a sense about the ongoing conflicts between Pakistan and India and Hindu and Muslims in the Kashmir region, because we included sources about these antagonisms in the previous source packets. And they have a vague notion about the tensions in the Mideast be-tween Israelis and Palestinians. But by and large, they remain ignorant about how these nations have developed over time and how these changes have af-fected peoples' cultural identities. Hence we attempt to respond to these ques-tions by concluding the course with a project revolving around the concept of development and its relationship to identity.

Just as people like you and me *develop* over time physically, mentally, emotionally, and spiritually, so too do nations in both material and nonmate-rial ways. People form egos and have self-images and so do nations. People mature, some more quickly than others, and so do nations, though I guess we could wonder what maturity really means. A nation's development results from the constant interplay among a wide variety of factors. The nature of this interplay is dynamic, and the change it brings can have an impact on the iden-tity and integrity of a culture. While working on the project, we hope that the students become exposed to these notions:

- that the concept of development includes many aspects beyond the economic and the political; among them are the spiritual, environ-mental, educational, artistic, and health-oriented;
- that all countries, not just so-called "Third World" nations, are devel-oping in one way or another at different stages and with different momentum;
- that the concept of development means change over time and not necessarily progress; thus progress remains in the eye of the beholder;
- that there are international institutions, which establish sets of criteria for development that need to be reexamined in light of individual na-tions' cultural identities;
- that development can be facilitated through cultural interaction;
- that development may come at a cost.

So what do we have the students do? After coming to some consensus in class about what factors are involved in a nation's development, each of the four student groups is responsible for putting together a packet of mate-rials—text, relevant maps, charts, data, etc.—drawn from research in the school library, which examines the present conditions and state of affairs of a certain country. We usually pick four countries that the students have en-countered during the course of the year, notably in their investigation of anticolonial movements for national independence. Group packets must also draw some conclusions about the level of development in their respec-tive countries at present and what the outlook is for future change. Packets must include a brief historical background of the country since achieving its independence. Students wrestle with such questions as, Are the criteria for development being met in your nation? Might your country be a model for development? Is it underdeveloped? After the packets are disseminated, each student for the final exam must complete the following task:

> You are a member of a Nobel Prize Committee that is about to award its annual prize for the "most developed nation." Given your understanding of the levels of development in each of the four nations under investigation, and given the impact of the changes upon their respective cultural identities, create your own definition of development, and then, using that definition, award the prize to the model country. You will need to rank order the four countries, and you will need to be able to defend your decision.

Thus, in this final unit of the course, we put students in the position of being citizens of the world, concerned with the world, or at least parts of it, in its present state. They have weighty judgments about what being *developed* or perhaps *modern* really means. Why are there so many poor people in the world? Why so much violence? Why so much disease? Are there universal human rights we can agree upon? At this final point in the school year, we are hopeful they have gained an appreciation for the importance of geographic and cultural perspective rooted in a world-historical context of cultural encounter and the changes wrought by these encounters.

Our world history survey is "not so ordinary" because we have chosen not to cover the entire history of humankind and therefore have deliberately left out much of the story. We have chosen not to bury our students under a heap of abstract concepts. We hope they might have some notion of why historians are so passionate about the study of history and how they go about their craft. In placing students in the role of historian, we challenge them to become more comfortable with ambiguity and uncertainty. We think that they will have become more sophisticated and inquisitive thinkers at the end of the year, and we would like to think that they have had some fun along the way. And finally, this world history survey is not so ordinary because it is constantly being reevaluated as new scholarship emerges about new ways of looking at the world and its past. Building a consensus among the staff in this endeavor is always a challenge but a healthy one. In Chapter 5 we will consider the future of world history teaching from a number of different angles.

Notes

1. William H. McNeill, "The World History Survey Course," quoted in Gilbert Allardyce, "Toward World History: American Historians and the Coming of the World History Course," in *Journal of World History* 1, no. 1 (Honolulu, 1990): 26.

2. William Swinton, *Outlines of World History,* quoted in Allardyce, 45.

3. Ibid., 47.

4. These "habits" are delineated quite effectively in the National Center for History in the Schools' *National Standards for History,* Basic Edition (Los Angeles: National Center for History in the Schools, 1996), 59–70. See also *Advanced Placement Course Description: World History* (Princeton, NJ: College Entrance Examination Board and Educational Testing Service, 2000).

5. Jay McTighe and Grant Wiggins, *The Understanding by Design Handbook* (Alexandria, VA: Association for Supervision and Curriculum Development, 1999), 37–45.

6. Ibid., 128.

7. See Gerard Danzer, *Mapping the World Geographic Frameworks for Global History* (Chicago: Windows to World History Project, University of Illinois at Chicago, 2000). There are several useful exercises in this booklet that focus on cartographic projections and perspectives.

8. Dennis Wood, "The Power of Maps," *Scientific American* (May 1993): 93.

9. Horace Miner, "Body Ritual Among the Nacirema," *American Anthropologist* 58 (1993): 503–507.

10. Ken Bischoff et al., "Power of Perspective: 'Map Projections'" (Princeton: *Pacesetter* World History Task Force, 1992).

11. Kevin Reilly, ed., *Readings in World Civilizations,* 3rd. ed., 2 vols. (New York: St. Martin's Press, 1995): 37–42.

12. These civilizations exist within empires—Greece during the golden age of Athens, India during Mauryan empire and Asoka's reign, China during the late Qin and Han Wu-di, and Rome during Augustus—which allow them to flourish and which permit contact and exchange of goods and ideas with outsiders as we shall see in the next group investigation.

13. Tom Martin, "Trade in the Indian Ocean: A Simulation Activity" (World History Association Summer Institute, San Francisco State University, 2000, photocopy), 1–12. Tom Martin, who teaches world history, led the Advanced Placement Institute.

14. The historian Lynda Shaffer has labeled the process by which the Southern and Eastern Hemispheres helped to ensure the economic development of first the Mediterranean and the rest of Europe, "Southernization." See Lynda Shaffer, "Southernization," *Journal of World History* 5, no. 1 (spring 1994): 1–21.

15. See, for example, the new prototype CD-ROM *Journeys Along the Silk Road,* by the Asia Society. Many of the primary sources, as they do for each of the group packets throughout the year, are drawn from various compilations. In terms of secondary sources, we have made use of Jerry Bentley's *Old World Encounters* and Daniel Boorstin's *The Discoverers.* See the resource list in the appendix.

16. Audrey Shabbas, *A Medieval Banquet in the Alhambra Palace* (Berkeley: AWAIR, 1993).

17. Teachers can consult sources listed in the appendix. In particular, the Mexican and Peruvian encounters draw heavily on Marvin Lunenfeld's *1492: Discovery, Invasion, Encounter. Sources and Interpretations*; the Canadian encounter on the film *Black Robe;* the Connecticut encounter on the Pequot War collection of documents—see Simulations in the appendix—and the Japanese encounter on David Lu's edited collection *Japan: A Documentary History*.

18. Some recent scholarship suggests the Equiano story is fictional, though it still can work well to elicit questions. See Olaudah Equaino, *The Interesting Narrative of the Life of Olaudah Equiano, or Gustavus Vassa, the African, Written by Himself*, 2 vols. (London, 1789). Another effective approach to engender such questions is to use the video *Black Sugar*, noted in the appendix, in which a Senegalese elder, perhaps a Griot, relates the slave trade experience to a young boy.

19. Alfred Andrea and James Overfield, eds. *The Human Record: Sources of Global History*, 3rd ed., vol. 1 (Boston: Houghton Mifflin, 1998), 459–61.

20. Cary Franklin, a Loomis Chaffee alumna, as part of an independent study with Mark Williams, created the role play. It is described in detail in Chapter 6.

21. For New York sources, see Peter Linebaugh and Marcus Rediker, *The Many-Headed Hydra: Sailors, Slaves, Commoners, and the Hidden History of the Revolutionary Atlantic* (Boston: Beacon Press, 2000), 174–210. For Brazilian sources, see among others, C. R. Boxer, *The Golden Age of Brazil, 1695–1750: Growing Pains of a Colonial Society* (New York: Palgrave, 1995).

22. See *The JVC Video Anthology of World Music and Dance*, prod. Ichikawa Katsumori, dir. Nakagawa Kunihiko, 30 vols., Victor Company of Japan, Inc., 1994, videocassettes. See also *The JVC and Smithsonian Folkways Video Anthology of Music and Dance of the Americas,* prod. Stephen McArthur, Multicultural Media, dir. Hiroaki Ohta, Smithsonian Folkways Recordings, 1995, videocassettes.

23. For sources on Haiti, see Julio Finn, *The Bluesman: The Musical Heritage of Black Men and Women in the Americas* (New York: Interlink Books, 1992), 6–37; Harold Courlander, *The Drum and the Hoe: Life and Lore of the Haitian People* (Berkeley: University of California Press, 1985), 1–7. See also the Manifesto of Henri Christophe in 1814, found in N. Wiesner et al., *Discovering the Global Past* (see appendix for full citation), and "The San Domingue Disturbances," Philadelphia *General Advertiser*, no. 351, 14 November 1791.

24. See John K. Thornton, "Dimensions of the Stono Rebellion," *American Historical Review* (October 1991): 158–70.

25. For an in-depth, penetrating, and still invaluable analysis of this mindset, see Edward Said, *Orientalism: Western Representations of the Orient* (New York: Random House, 1978).

26. See in particular the essay by the Indian historian, L. M. Panikkar, "World War I in World History," in Kevin Reilly, ed., *Readings in World Civilizations*, vol. 2 (full citation in appendix).

27. These packets are created from a variety of source readers including Johnson, Johnson, and Clark *Through Indian Eyes* Clark, *Through African Eyes;* and Pearson and Clark, *Through Middle Eastern Eyes;* and *The Human Record* (full citations listed in appendix).

2

"We're Making History"
Designing a Curriculum for Sixth Graders

LOU RATTÉ

What should be the shape and content of a world history course for sixth graders? What subjects should it cover? How will the subjects be linked? What scholarship will we draw upon? What will be the goals? These were the motivating questions in a six-year-long project in social studies reform in which I took part.[1] During the lifetime of the project some three hundred people collaborated in the process and final completion of the written version of the curriculum. These included teachers, school administrators, project staff, scholars from area colleges and universities, members of the state Geographic Alliance and the state Writing Project, museum and arts educators and museum curators, dance consultants, curriculum specialists, and pedagogic experts. First as the project's outside evaluator, then as the project scholar, and finally as the editor and author of the written version of the curriculum, I was one of the collaborators. My job was to see that all the contributions fit together, that the students would be learning history, and that the curriculum would be non-Eurocentric.

Although university scholars have played a role in projects such as this, it is a fuzzy one, not well articulated. There is no model for how the scholar collaborator should proceed other than the sense, as the cliché goes, that "scholars know what to teach and teachers know how to teach." Since the 1980s, when a new generation of educational reformers began to take notice of American students' apparent lack of historical knowledge, there have been attempts both in and outside the historical profession to right the perceived wrongs of what happened decades ago when social studies replaced history in the schools. In many of these efforts the aim has been to enrich the teachers'

39

knowledge base. Many have been encouraging models of successful collaboration, while others have been fraught with problems.

In our project the positive far outweighed the negative, though, in the enthusiasm that project participants had for the idea of collaboration. Because of the duration of our project, and the serious and long-term commitment that many of the collaborators made, we were able to address some of the issues that need to be addressed if we are to work out the relationship that ought to exist between scholarship and what is taught in our classrooms.

The 1980s was a fruitful if combative time to address issues involving the relationship between research knowledge and classroom content. Not only was it a time when historians were recognizing the need to play a more responsible role in teaching beyond their own research areas, but the efforts of many young historians to search out the pasts and experiences of those who had been under- or unrepresented in the historical record were bearing fruit. This new scholarship helped spark the "culture wars," with advocates for multiculturalism on one side of the divide, and upholders of the canon on the other. While "multicultural" tended to be the key adjective in reform efforts in American history, "non-Eurocentric" was the watchword directing attention away from the European survey and toward world history.

I joined the Hartford project after several important steps had been taken. The group of planners, made up of the project directors, teachers, administrators, scholars, and arts representatives, had already decided that the world history curriculum for the sixth grade would focus on cities, and they had chosen the six cities to be included. The choice of these particular cities was the planners' way of asserting that the curriculum would be non-Eurocentric, and that it would at least move in the direction of being representative of the student body it was meant to serve. In addition to starting with the students' own city, Hartford, it would include Timbuktu in Africa, San Juan in Puerto Rico, two cities in Asia (Banaras and Tokyo), and Athens in Europe. Finally, all the planners assumed that the guiding discipline for the curriculum would be history, and that material from the arts would be fully integrated into it.

None of us who worked on the curriculum after these decisions had been made, at least as far as I know, challenged the planners' choices. I found it exciting and intellectually stimulating to work with others toward producing a world history curriculum that would weave together these six cities in some historically coherent way and that would, to the best of our knowledge and ability, be non-Eurocentric. During the six years while we were working on the curriculum, I learned a good deal about these six cities and the regions in which they are found, their histories with their moments of glory, and their apparent sagas of decline into historical obscurity. I came to appreciate some of what was involved in exploring ways of seeing that could be called non-Eurocentric. And I had a lot of time and opportunity to explore how scholarly knowledge can play a part in school curricula.

Coherence: Hartford, The Students' Own City

"Cities: Windows on the World" was a large and long-term project and many people worked on it during the course of its development from an idea to a written, textbook-style curriculum, complete with teacher's guide and student course book. Each unit in the curriculum is devoted to one of the six cities and consists of from five to ten lessons. Each includes detailed suggestions on how the unit can be taught, how much time the teacher should expect to spend on each lesson, where problems might arise, and what choices there are for shortening or expanding the unit. These suggestions were developed by a group of teachers working with a curriculum specialist at the time when the final version of the curriculum was being put together.

My role had been to shape the lessons into a coherent historical sequence, to facilitate the transition from one city to the next, and to provide an introductory unit to the whole curriculum. This role had evolved over time and in response to the testing of various curriculum drafts produced in collaborative summer institutes. While enthusiasm for the institutes was generally very high, many teachers found themselves adrift when it came to teaching. Not only was it difficult for teachers to move from one city to the next, it was often a problem, at the early stages of curriculum development, to move from one lesson to the next. Initially, teachers were responsible for creating the curriculum, and they had at their disposal a huge array of collaborators' contributions. For each of the six cities there was at least one scholar, either an area studies specialist or, if we were very lucky, someone who had actually studied the history of the particular city. There were dance consultants and arts consultants for each city, and there were graduate student "gofers" assigned to collect student-friendly sources relating to the cities. There was, in short, a mountain of potential material; but how did it fit together?

Had we been introducing teachers to a textbook, of course, the problems would have been vastly different, and probably a good deal easier to solve. All textbooks, even the bad ones, incorporate some form of conceptualization that enables a user of the book to move forward from page one through to the end. How were our teachers to move forward? How were they to know at the beginning of the year where they might be at the end? How should lessons and units hang together? How could this mass of material be given disciplinary integrity? In short, how could it be organized as history? How the first unit took shape will provide the example.

The Hartford unit opens with a lesson focusing on the students themselves, within their own city, their neighborhood. Teachers who worked on the lesson with consultants from the Geographic Alliance were wonderfully inventive in working out ways students could analyze the city. In a lesson titled "The Geography of Me," students started with their house and were taught how to plot distances from house to house, corner to corner, house to shops, shops to school, house to school, and so on. They had instructions on how to make family trees and conduct interviews with family members, neighbors, shopkeepers, and teachers. They even had suggestions on how to take and interpret photographs and other kinds of family memorabilia. Evidence had to be collected and then put together in the form of a "Community Analysis," a descriptive and interpretive account of the neighborhood and its surrounds.

The lesson was a model of coherence. The assessment exercise, the "Community Analysis," was to be given out at the start of the lesson, enabling teachers and students to know at the beginning where they would be expected to be at the end, aware that they had a variety of available choices on how to get there.

Could the whole of the curriculum be this good? How was it to be organized so that teachers would know at the beginning, of each lesson, each unit, and of the course as a whole, where they would be likely to be at the end? How would we embody the desired goals of combining age-appropriate skill-oriented lessons with intellectually sound historical concepts and materials?

The scholarly contribution to the Hartford unit had been to call attention to changes in the city in the course of the twentieth century through focusing on a particular street which was torn down in the 1970s to make way for a large urban renewal project. Primary and secondary sources were plentiful, depicting the life of the street, Front Street, when it had been home to immigrants newly arrived in the city. We had oral histories, before-and-after photographs, and several powerful lectures describing and analyzing economic change in the twentieth century. For the study of the urban renewal project, called Constitution Plaza, we had an equally large body of sources, including newspaper reports, taped interviews with participants in the project and observers, promotional brochures, feature articles, and the like.

We had ample material to show that change had taken place, not only in the city's economy, but in the very fabric of the city. Hartford in 1990 did not look like Hartford in 1920. The goal was to engage students (and teachers) in the study of change, but how could we make these changes comprehensible and interesting to students in the time allowed for teaching the unit?

The question had large ramifications. As my own role became more directive I had to ask: how was I going to understand change in this context in ways that would prove useful throughout the whole curriculum? What particular historical approach should be introduced at this early point in the curriculum, and how should it be related to the common human story the whole-year curriculum was supposed to tell?

In one of those strokes of genius that happens in collaborative projects, our director decided to make buttons for all project members: students, teachers, and collaborators. Inscribed on the buttons was the legend: "We're Making History." Here was the point: people make history (even if not always in circumstances of their own choosing!). Introducing human agency into students' understanding of the past was to become a central aim of the whole curriculum.

With questions of agency in mind, we asked: who initiates change on such a massive and public scale as happened in Hartford in the 1960s and 1970s? What motivates such people? In what specific historical circumstances do they operate? What resources do they command in order to carry out the changes they deem necessary or desirable?

I had freedom to address these questions in ways that I saw fit, and often the best way was to turn to additional research in order to find the means to contextualize a particular issue or event. To address questions of agency in the urban renewal movement in the 1960s and 1970s, I went back to the City Beautiful movement in Hartford at the turn of the twentieth century. According to its interpreters, this urban renewal movement was initiated by self-styled city fathers in order to create visual and architectural means to Americanize the new immigrant population that was pouring into Hartford from southern, eastern, and central Europe. Front Street was the first place of residence for new immigrants, the place where people first established some sense of community in their new country. Front Street residents in the early 1900s would have been prime targets for the City Beautiful planners who no doubt knew the immigrants' lives were hard but who nonetheless thought they should be exposed to beauty as a means for acquiring virtue, as they passed through the public buildings of their state capitol.

City Beautiful planners were certainly aware of change in their city, and it was change they did not like and sought to control. They expressed negative opinions about the new immigrants swelling Hartford's population; but they believed in the power of art to effect changes in behavior and demeanor. They purposefully changed the way the city looked with the goal of making its inhabitants more virtuous. Were ideas like these operative in the 1960s? Or did the city planners who tore down Front Street have other beliefs and motives? Both groups of planners felt they could make decisions that would affect the lives of other people. Did they have the same motivation?

This became the question to answer as students worked through the source materials. There was one interesting twist in the sources that checked the easy judgment that whereas City Beautiful planners had presented themselves as the benefactors of the poor, the builders of Constitution Plaza had simply wanted to get the poor out of sight. Front Street, so several sources suggested, was the first residence of newly arrived immigrants, the poorest section of town, and the place you definitely wanted to leave as soon as economic opportunity enabled you to get out. Residents who had to move out to make way for the new construction of Constitution Plaza were compensated, and there was no apparent outcry of protest at the heartlessness of city leaders.

Historians always need to be concerned with who is doing the acting and under what circumstances. To provide a context for urban renewal in the 1960s, I found it useful to go back to an earlier time in the history of the city when, as in the 1960s, city leaders acted in what seemed like their own interest, but with the sense that they would be helping their city. By setting the urban renewal movement of the 1960s in relation to the City Beautiful movement more than a half century earlier, we provided the Hartford unit with three components of historical inquiry: (1) there is a persistent context, meaning not simply the city but decision making in the city; (2) the study of decision making moves through time; and (3) the sources allow for interpretations about how and why changes in the very fabric of the city occur.

Foundational Subjects: Athens, the Teachers' Choice

Athens was included in the "Cities" curriculum because teachers already taught about it and no one thought it should be left out, no matter how strong the desire to be non-Eurocentric. Banaras had been suggested by the initial planning board as the site for teaching about mythology, but the potential allure of the Sanskrit epics *Mahabharata* and *Ramayana* was simply not strong enough to unseat Zeus, Hera, Athena, and all the rest. Athens, and the accoutrements it has acquired as a foundational subject, emerged in the first draft of the curriculum as a monument to a much loved part of our own national life.

The first draft of the Athens unit still occupies a very special place for me because, starting out as the project evaluator, I had to pass judgment on it. It stood on my desk as a towering pile, dwarfing the tiny Timbuktu and Banaras collections, practically obscuring Tokyo and San Juan, and even a good inch higher than the unit on the students' own city, Hartford. What was in that mass of material?

Some of the procedures adopted early on in the project now appear to all of us to have been ludicrous: how could we ever have thought the one I am about to describe would work? While teachers attended the presentations by scholar consultants, graduate students were sent out to collect materials on the city in question. Not unpredictably, the materials thus collected often had no bearing at all on what the scholars had said. We abandoned this practice after the first year, but in that first year it served to provide visual proof of an obvious condition of scholarly endeavor: different subjects are studied differently, and some are studied more than others. I use the word "studied" here with caution: material that can be collected on Athens, in contrast, say, to material on Banaras, is much more a demonstration of the city's status as foundational subject than of the ways in which it is constituted in academic discourse. That said, it is often this very material that is most accessible to teachers: pictures of the Acropolis, Greek statuary, and black and red figure vases; lavishly illustrated versions of Greek mythology; tales of Athens and Sparta; picture books on the Olympic games; concept-related presentations on Greek democracy; Greek theater; and the like.

Athens has been so well established as a foundational subject in our elementary curriculum, our textbooks, and our surveys, that you tamper with it at your own risk. Even the most diehard of non-Eurocentric multiculturalists at the height of enthusiasm for the multicultural curriculum would not think of removing it from study altogether. For veteran teachers and even for novices, Athens is so familiar, so comfortable, and yes, so necessary. At the very least it represents a large dose of our national cultural literacy. Of course we can't do without it. In the "Cities" curriculum it stands forth as "the birthplace of democracy." The Athens unit has lessons on Greek vases and Greek architecture, Greek assemblies, the Athenian ideal, Greek imperialism, and the Olympic games. The unit is rich with primary documents, glossaries, visual guides, and practical directions on how to build a shoe box Parthenon and a post-and-lintel structure.

My contribution to the shaping of the unit was to give it a theme: continuity. By shaping the lessons in certain ways, I meant to convey that there was a relationship between the previous unit, Hartford, and this one. We do connect with this ancient city in unique ways; why is that so? What is it about Athens that makes knowing about it seem so inevitable? It is the place where, at least until recently, we used to begin our surveys (with brief nods to Egypt and Babylon) starting in elementary school and going right through college, the place to which we trace our political and cultural roots. How all that came to be seems worth thinking about, and how to begin to think about it can connect us to a good deal of current scholarship and debate.

Students are encouraged to begin their study of Athens with maps, time lines, and a skills review: what is the distance from Hartford to Athens? What are the physical obstacles a traveler would have to surmount in order to go from Hartford to Athens today? one hundred years ago? (trick question) five

hundred years ago? one thousand years ago? How much time has elapsed between the time when Athens was at its peak and today? What has happened in
those 2,500 years?

The unit provides a simple time line that presents major historical periodizations and then focuses on Hartford: Classical Athens, Imperial Rome,
the Medieval period, the Renaissance, the early modern period, the beginnings of European expansion, the Scientific Revolution and the Enlightenment, English settlement in Connecticut (the students' home state), the
American revolution and establishment of a democratic government, the
Greek revival in architecture in Hartford.

The purpose of both the map exercise and the exercise with the time line
is to establish distance between the Athens of the classical period and the
Hartford of the students' own time, to suggest that people in Hartford must
have had to make some choices at some time in their own history in order
to have Athens occupy the place it does in our consciousness today. We
don't have to introduce the term "invention of tradition" to young students
in order to encourage them to think about why knowing about Athens is a
good thing.

At the early stages of curriculum development, when we were introducing maps in the earlier grades, some teachers remarked that we were asking
students to do complicated analyses when they didn't even know the directions. The answer was simple enough: teach them where north is, where south
is, where east and west are; and review, and drill, until they are comfortable
with those conventions. What is true of cartographic conventions is true of
chronological conventions, time lines, periodization. As students use the map
to identify physical obstacles between themselves and Athens, they are encouraged to use the time line to identify potential chronological obstacles.
Hmmm; maybe people in Hartford really became interested in Athens when
Americans established their own democracy. It's a beginning.

Technically speaking, I was encouraging historicizing: when and under
what conditions does a particular idea, belief, or event in the past become important to a group? Connecting the consensus of what we should know about
Athens to the unit on Hartford immediately preceding the Athens unit
seemed to me to be the key to maintaining the sense of agency introduced in
the first unit and to reinforce the historical narrative in which Hartford was
presented. The unit does not attempt to present Athenian history. It rather encourages us to address this question: what does Athens represent to us?

In working out how the question might be raised, I used the lesson on
vases, provided by one of our museum collaborators. Students can only profit
from being able to recognize and describe the variety of shapes, functions, and
decorative motifs on black and red figure vases. Many children love to pose in

the archaic posture of sixth-century vases and are remarkably adept at reading the more complicated narratives on vases of the classical period. It does
not take away from their delight, after the museum visit, to show pictures of
what they saw and to encourage them to wonder how the objects got into the
museum in the first place. Were these objects handed down in families from
parent to child, as great treasures? How do we happen to have them in our
own museum? Where have they been during those 2,500 years? Did the first
settlers bring them over in their luggage?

From these questions, which, of course, are meant to whet curiosity
rather than be answered, we move on to others. Why did people in Hartford
build buildings that looked like Greek buildings? Is our government really like
the government of the Greeks in fifth-century b.c.e. Athens? For teachers,
why should we not talk about and even teach about the markers of Athenian
greatness while at the same time speculating on why they are regarded as great
in our society? In other words, why not inquire into why and how foundational subjects achieve that status?

In 1990 none of us were sure about just what "non-Eurocentric," or, for
that matter, "Eurocentric," might mean. I interpreted the planners' mandate
to mean that the curriculum should not have the European historical narrative at the center with other areas of the world tacked on when they came in
contact with Europe; and that the curriculum should incorporate new scholarship on areas of the world outside Europe and America. It was not clear
to me in 1990 how scholarly endeavor would explore ever more intricately
how a Eurocentric view of the world came into being; what was clearer was
that a Eurocentric view not only focused on Europe as the center of a world-
historical narrative, but posited that it was Europeans who had the say when
it came to defining peoples from elsewhere. A non-Eurocentric approach, then,
would have to include letting others have their own say. Non-Eurocentric
would also mean raising questions that would help us understand the European perspective, especially in so far as we all share that perspective. Through
encouraging questions about why Greek vases occupy prestigious places in
our museums, I wanted to open up for questioning why we, specifically, think
knowing about them is important. In raising these questions I was drawing on
a growing body of critical literature on museum practice. This literature examines ethnographic collecting and exhibiting in a context that includes European colonial expansion and the beginnings of anthropological inquiry. It
explores how it is that some objects (Greek vases, for instance) are presented
in museums as art while others, most commonly objects from outside Europe
and America, are presented as examples of culture. At the root of this new
object-focused scholarship is movement within several disciplines to go to the
roots of how our academic disciplines themselves became Eurocentric.

Was it my concern with the problem of Eurocentrism or teacher devotion to the subject that played the larger role in shaping the Athens unit? The latter, surely. Probably all teachers, especially those long practiced in the profession, have their favorite subjects: ones that the teacher can see coming with that sense of expectation and pleasure that the memory of past experiences with students and the anticipation of learning still more about a much loved subject brings. For many teachers Athens is such a subject. The comfort level in teaching about Athens is high and there is no problem about how to assess student learning: teachers know what to expect of their students in the matter of demonstration, and they know what they want their students to learn.

They also know what they don't want to include. One of our scholar collaborators made a lengthy and lively presentation on Greek homoeroticism and its role in Athenian life, to a polite, interested, but ultimately dismissive audience.

Teacher Collaboration: Banaras, India's Holy City

I liked working on this unit the most. The history of India is my own area of scholarly specialization, I worked with a good friend of mine on the unit, and during the six years while we were all working on the curriculum I was spending a part of every year in India on my own research. During one of those periods I went to Banaras, took photographs, and bought posters for the project. For me it was a time of tremendous learning. I was trying to bring to bear on my own work some of the critical and theoretical perspectives that were shaping the scholarship of many; and I was learning a good deal about how to, and how not to, approach Indian history before the coming of the British in the light of scholarly critiques of historical knowledge. Similarly, I was learning about the importance of situating oneself in the present in order to approach the immediate colonial past, which was my subject. In short, I was learning something about what should and should *not* be in a curriculum on India for American students. Something about India today must be included; that India is remote and spiritually obsessed should be left out.

Time for teaching any one of the six units making up the "Cities" curriculum is limited, and for each city we had to provide a context that would enable teachers to begin. We tried to build each city into an appropriate historical context, given that each was studied at a specific time period: Hartford in the twentieth century; Athens in the fifth century B.C.E.; Timbuktu in the fourteenth and fifteenth centuries; San Juan in its Spanish colonial period, from the early sixteenth century to 1898. Banaras was the exception. No particular time period or event stood out. Recognizing that teachers felt they knew little or nothing about India to begin with, our first scholar consultant presented an array of tourist literature and popular images, along with more serious teaching materials, in the hope of creating the comfort level from which teachers could go forward to set their own learning agendas. This strategy backfired when teachers took the promotional literature to be itself adequate for teaching. What was emerging, in the first attempt at making the curriculum, was India as cliché, not, to be sure, as land of poverty, overpopulation, and caste rigidity, but as site of ancient wisdom, mystery, and exotic spirituality. In other words, India was emerging as marked by difference from us.

We obviously did not want Banaras to serve as the gateway for reinforcing popular American stereotypes about India. Even articulating that position, however, was problematic and instructive: at one of the follow-up sessions I was making a long speech about not perpetuating stereotypes about all Indians being religious when one of the teachers interrupted to ask, "How do we know that's a stereotype?" Very good question. Indeed, how do we deal with what Americans *already know* about India in order to make way for what we could know if we turned to the scholarship? The issue touched directly on how we were going to interpret *multiculturalism* and *non-Eurocentrism,* two terms given to us in the planners' mandate. Multiculturalism had already been trivialized into what critics called the "grass skirts" approach, in which unfamiliar parts of the world were presented through representations of practices most distant from the late twentieth-century United States. Multiculturalism was most vulnerable to slippage into issues of self-esteem, cultural relativism, and overly simplistic arguments for why everyone should respect everyone else's culture. The words of one of our evaluators were instructive here: if you can teach what you want to teach in a woodworking course, you shouldn't call it history.

To guard against slippage of this sort we wanted to introduce material on Banaras that would come from the world of contemporary scholarship. This ruled out presenting the city through the lens of recent urban history since, as far as we were able to find out, Banaras hasn't been studied under that rubric. We could have presented the city through the theme of civilizational or cultural contact, since there is plenty of material on eighteenth- and nineteenth-century British responses to and descriptions of Banaras, but such an approach didn't seem to get at the heart of what was most interesting about the city, and, indeed, what most struck a visitor. Using as our major source Harvard scholar Diana Eck's book *Banaras, City of Light*.[2] This, after all, is the way it is seen by the many who come to it every year. As a sacred city, Banaras is timeless, sacred space constructed out of texts, memories, and inspired imagination as much as it is out of stones and brick. Eck presents the city in its manifestation as sacred space, the place to which pilgrims come and perform acts appropriate to being there. You don't just come to Banaras. You do something there. Here we had our organizing principle: students would come to Banaras as pilgrims, and do what pilgrims do there. Adopting this principle allowed for the development of a number of student activities (role playing, storytelling, holding a fair [*mela*]) and allowed us to incorporate a number of different primary sources, textual and visual.

The use of identifying themes for each city, which grew out of the materials as they were put together, was proving to have an added payoff. Not only did these themes help as organizing devices for the separate units, but they also seemed general enough to apply to all the cities. We thus began the Banaras unit urging students to recognize that belief seems to be a universal in human societies. What people believe may well be different the world over, but that they believe it seems safe to say. How do we know? How do people express their beliefs? In the Banaras unit we are not interested in *what* pilgrims believe; we are interested in how they express their beliefs. To my mind, the hero of the unit is a boy, Mandapa, who makes his entrance in one of the stories that Eck quotes. Mandapa is a bad boy who betrays his friends. In return, they beat him up and leave him for dead. When Mandapa wakes up he is afraid to go back to family and friends, and sees a band of pilgrims passing by. He decides to join them and lose himself in the crowd. Mandapa knows nothing about gods and goddesses and festivals but in order to escape detection under his new cover, he does what the pilgrims around him are doing. So earnest does he become in this desire not to be singled out that he actually becomes the exemplary pilgrim, and achieves liberation. I imagined that students would so enjoy the activities associated with the pilgrimage that they would not have to ask what it all meant, and no teacher would be made to feel the need to speak with authority on what Hindus believe.

Since Indians recognize six seasons to our four, we organized the unit into six lessons, starting each with a quote from a poem by the great Gupta period dramatist, Kalidasa, on the seasons. Each lesson drew attention to a festival celebrated in Banaras during that season. In connection with the festival, there were stories to be told, gods and goddesses to be introduced, vocabulary to be learned, and a practical activity. In early spring, for instance, students were encouraged to make a mural of the river bank, using photographs by one of India's great, and recently deceased, photographers, Raghubir Singh. In the hot season they were encouraged to write a praise poem on the order of the *mahatmyas*, or praise songs exaggerating the merits of the person being honored. Rainy season was the time for telling stories, holding fairs, honoring snakes by drawing pictures of them and hanging them out for display, and showing devotion to friends by tying brightly colored wrist bands around their wrists. Hanuman, Rama's loyal monkey general from *Ramayana*, is a favorite of this season, as is Ravana, the demon who becomes his antagonist in the battle to recapture Sita. Here are multiple possibilities for telling stories, acting out episodes from *Ramayana*, drawing illustrations, and the like.

So it was with all the seasons: students could make clay pots in autumn to honor Durga and little clay lamps to celebrate Divali, the festival of lights; in the cold season they could honor Ganesh, the elephant-headed son of Siva whose special role is to remove obstacles, and Saraswati, the goddess of learning. Cold season is also the time when Mandapa makes his ultimately successful pilgrimage. Finally, in spring, student pilgrims can celebrate Sivaratri with the telling of stories about the great god Siva, and Holi, when there is dancing and playing in the streets and people reverse roles, with servants and workers taking on the part of masters and bosses, students taking on the role of teachers.

I had imagined that this unit would be one of the more exciting and colorful, one in which teachers might engage with the same kind of open-ended enthusiasm that moved the students. The unit had rich visual materials, including classical images of Siva and popular posters of all the deities present in Banaras, and students loved them. We also had two dance collaborators for the unit. I thought, the only problem with this unit is that teachers will want to teach it all year!

We ran self-evaluation study groups during the year for teachers who had been introduced to the curriculum in summer institutes and were piloting the unit. It was with astonishment and chagrin that I read teacher reports on how they were using the unit. One teacher had found it necessary to start the unit with a lesson on the great religions of the world and what their adherents believed in order to address the question of what Hinduism was, and several other teachers had started out with Martin Luther King and Gandhi. What went wrong?

I am not sure what went wrong, and I am still unsure about the question of background information necessary for teaching about areas of the world outside Europe and the United States. What I did learn from the experience of reading the teacher self-evaluations was the important reminder that we all do start with what we know when we encounter the new and unfamiliar. And only after immersion in the subject do we discover the questions that are really worth asking. In working on the Banaras unit I had indulged myself and I was able to imagine doing all the wonderful things the curriculum suggested because, in fact, I had already done many of them and observed or participated in others. I had written the curriculum for myself; I wanted to be studying it. As a person with a long and abiding interest in India but nonetheless a foreigner, I could identify with Mandapa, the bad boy who knew nothing but was nonetheless liberated.

I approve of passion in learning, even my own, for which I have had to develop some tolerance; but I discovered that while it may be possible for some people to communicate passion, it is not so easy to communicate experience. Scholarship today on areas once directly colonized by European states or brought under the cultural influence of Europe and the United States is permeated with challenges to our objective ways of knowing, summed up in these examples by the teacher who began the Banaras unit with introductory material on the great religions of the world. Only a long way into the subject do we discover the problems with starting with general statements about what other people believe and do with their lives. In designing the Banaras unit I had hoped to bypass the problem of introductory knowledge by moving students right into the center of the pilgrim's life, with no explanatory information provided. It did not work. Teachers felt that India was strange, distant, and unfathomable. In the end many did not choose to keep India and Banaras separate, and fell back upon generalizations and stereotypes. One teacher, long experienced in working with children, however, did show how the unit could be taught without challenging the integrity of the students and their own experience. In her assessment exercise, at the end of the cold season when the pilgrims and Mandapa completed their pilgrimage to the holy places around the city, she asked the students to decide whether they would bathe in the Ganges. They were, after all, visitors to Banaras, guests of the holy city, still Americans. What would *they* do?

Outside Collaborators: Timbuktu

The question of how to work in all the rich material from outside collaborators remained difficult to answer throughout the project, but one which I eventually felt called for ingenuity in the service of historical coherence. For instance, for the Banaras unit we had the opportunity to incorporate visual materials on Chola bronze representations of Siva, including the famous and familiar Siva Nataraj, and one of our dance collaborators involved students in a dance about Lord Krishna, one of the few deities in the Hindu pantheon who does not have a major role in Banaras. To simply add these wonderfully enriching materials without explanation to a unit focusing specifically on Banaras would give students the wrong message and reinforce the temptation many teachers had to use Banaras as an entry to teach about India.

The device was simple enough: as the student pilgrims are leaving Banaras, at the end of their pilgrimage year, they make two side trips, one to the old capital of the Chola Empire where they learn about the workshop of the Queen under whose patronage the Siva Nataraj was actually invented, and another to Brindavan, the home of Lord Krishna. Devices such as these are indeed simple enough, and they can play an important role in encouraging the kind of attentiveness that can eventually make us more sensitive to voices other than our own.

In the case of the Timbuktu unit, the problem was to find a way to connect what many teachers already did in teaching about Africa to lessons focusing on Timbuktu from the thirteenth to the sixteenth centuries. At the time when our project's original planners chose Timbuktu as one of the six cities to be studied in the "Cities" world history curriculum, there was already a great deal of curricular information available on Africa's three great medieval empires, Ghana, Mali, and Songhai. There was also a good deal of material for elementary school students on African *Griots* (oral historians, storytellers) and African folktales. Many teachers had already incorporated material on the three empires into their curricula, and most used folktales in some way.

The Timbuktu unit focused on the city in the context of the three great empires. The unit included background information drawn from conceptual knowledge about early urban development (material on food surplus, division of labor, access to transportation as prerequisites for urban growth); an introduction to the role of Islam in the region; time lines for the sequence of empires; and the presentation of the city as a center of trade and Islamic learning.

My contribution to this basic frame was to add material on the difficulty of sources surviving in the desert climate and the necessity of relying on Islamic historians, geographers, and travelers in making ancient Timbuktu known outside West Africa. I also added material on what the Romans knew about sub-Saharan Africa and the gold trade. The original draft introduced the camel as "the ship of the desert" and I added materials on when the camel is supposed to have reached Africa. I found out that the camel is thought to have originated in North America, and to have walked over the same land mass traversed by people of Central Asia who walked in the other direction to become America's First Peoples. The image is captivating: people are going one way, and camels are going the other. Camels, I thought, would be something of a "hook," a natural to keep student interest.

Similarly, I added material on what has been called "dumb barter." We first hear about "dumb barter" in Herodotus, who apparently heard about it from someone claiming to know something about the West African gold trade. Two groups of people approach a river bank from different directions. One leaves goods and departs. The other comes up, inspects the goods, and leaves a pile of gold, then departs. The first returns, inspects the pile, and if it seems like a good price, takes the gold and heads home. If the price is too low, he (in the story they are probably all men) goes back again without taking the gold. The other person returns and adds to the pile of gold. When the price is settled, each party takes what he wants and leaves the scene.

From Herodotus' time on, various people have commented on dumb barter (or "the silent trade") in West Africa. It seemed like another "hook" and I asked our consulting scholar about it. He asked me to consider whether I thought trade in that manner was actually likely, with no one speaking, perhaps with the suggestion that one party, at least, is incapable of learning the language of the other. Might there not be some obvious bias built into the representation? In many of the Islamic sources it is clear that the Arabs who crossed the desert to trade with the West Africans thought they were bringing civilization to these peoples who had no religion of the book. I wrote up the lesson to include both the stories about dumb barter and the question about bias in the sources.

Overall, the Timbuktu unit made the point that trade was important in the development of these empires. We introduced material from French archaeological finds at Khoumbi, an eleventh-century site in ancient Ghana, reporting on the presence of iron nails, knives, scissors, farming tools, glass weights for measuring gold, Mediterranean pottery, and stones with Koranic inscriptions. We had textual and visual sources showing the trade in salt, and of course we had materials on the gold trade. In sketchy and summary fashion, we carried the story of Timbuktu up to 1592, when it was invaded by Moroccans. It then drops from the historical record, only to become, in our own day, the nowhere to which we go "from here . . ."

Although this sketchy history of the city whets one's appetite for knowing more about the history of the region in the pre-European period, our primary role was accomplished: Timbuktu stands in the curriculum as a corrective to the view that nothing happened in Africa from the time of the first emergence of humans until the arrival of European traders and imperialists.

Teacher interest in the unit did not stop with trade and Islamic learning before 1592, however. Many teachers had already incorporated material on Griots and from African folktales into their social studies work, and they knew that this material worked well with students. How did such material fit with what we had put together on the three great empires? To include material the source for which we could not identify would be to encourage the homogenization of "Africa" as a cultural monolith, and work against the goals of the project for creating a history curriculum.

We had used Arab sources in the construction of the unit. Arab historians, beginning with the eleventh-century Al-Bakri, who had never actually been to Timbuktu but had used material from Arab travelers to write about the city, had a well-developed professional tradition by the time they were writing about Islam in West Africa. As people of the Book, and as people who believed that Islam was a civilizing force in West Africa, they would probably not have rated Griots at the court of the emperors very highly, or as comparable to themselves in their capacity as historians. One source bore out this hypothesis. Its author disparaged the activity of the court Griot, but in doing so at least acknowledged his presence. If we could say that there were Griots in Timbuktu in our time period, we could have them in the curriculum. These devices of legitimation may seem torturous, but I felt it important that the written document, meant to serve teachers as a resource for years to come, maintain its historical integrity.

In "Cities" I did not attempt to bring in, in a direct way, any of the critiques of historical practice that have been produced in the wake of scholarly critiques of European imperialism. What I did attempt to do, as part of the effort to be non-Eurocentric, was to try to avoid continuing practices that scholarship had called into question. Since the early 1980s anthropologists have been calling attention to the central role that their discipline has played in representing places outside Europe and United States as timeless and unchanging societies. In this scenario, only the West has history. We know this division best in the dyad tradition and modernity, with the latter term reserved only for Europe and America until the era of European expansion and imperialism, when the benevolent West brings the rest of the world into the modern era.

Recognizing these critiques and their ramifications for the presentation of survey knowledge can help to shape curriculum by sending up warning flags, such as the warning to resist the temptation to generalize about all of Africa through time. What I discovered in the project, however, was that the warning flag of contemporary scholarship could conflict with the goal of multiculturalism. Presenting Griots as the historians of Africa served what in 1990 seemed a worthy purpose, that of demonstrating that Europeans were not the only ones who had historians.

Including material on Anansi tales, dilemma tales, and Griots enabled teachers to talk about values in African societies, which many wanted to be able to do. To counter-balance this material, I wondered, might we then include material that showed contemporary Africans reflecting on their region's past? I drew on work done by Susan Vogel at the Museum for African Art in New York to find reproductions of paintings showing contemporary West African painters representing Islamic subjects, colonial subjects, and modernity. For the first, we had Senegalese paintings of the Kaaba, Islamic Holy Men, a Koranic school, and a Marabout. For the colonial period, we had narrative paintings done by artists from Congo depicting European colonialism; and for modernity we had a representation of Holy man riding in a car, an abstract cityscape, and a symbolist representation of villagers watching television.

I had learned, in connection with my own work in India, the importance of dealing with the present whenever you are presenting a part of the world with which the audience is unfamiliar. Because of the pervasiveness in our society of ideas about the "non-West," that is, of stereotypes that we don't even recognize as stereotypes, and because of the still persistent ways of presenting the rest of the world as timeless, changeless, and traditional, many Americans simply have no idea about the present of such world areas as India or the modern countries of Africa. It was, in fact, to this very idea of the traditional as characteristic of the rest of the world that every market multiculturalism appealed.

The incorporation into the Timbuktu unit of visual images by contemporary West African artists made the points that Africans today are the products of the past (as we all are); that the past includes the presence of Islam in West Africa; that most of the entire continent was colonized by Europeans; and that Africans today reflect upon their past, as we do here in America. The narrative paintings of colonial subjects helped to make the point that what happened in between Timbuktu in the 1300s and 1400s and today lies the period of European conquest. We ended the lesson, which included the images, with materials that summed up the changes in trade occasioned by the coming of Europeans to the Atlantic coast of West Africa. Most young students today know something about the slave trade. The curriculum offered a view of a specific area in West Africa before the development of the Atlantic slave trade, and, through the presentation of the visual images, a sense of what came to the continent with the coming of the Europeans, concluding with the sense that people who are living full and complex lives are reflecting on their past in ways accessible to us.

The inclusion of the arts in school curricula has generally been at the enrichment or illustrative levels. In "Cities" there were many occasions when we worked with collaborators who wanted us to continue these practices. Because the mandate was to work toward being non-Eurocentric, and because scholarship was helpful in our understanding of what non-Eurocentric could mean at the intellectual level, we worked at creating a new model, that of full integration. With such a model in mind, the questions changed. For instance, when we worked in a lesson on African dance, we did not ask what African dance was, but rather, how does the study of African dance address the issues our curriculum wants to address?

The lesson on African dance began with directions to the students to instruct the dance teacher in what they have learned about Timbuktu. Student preparation for their meeting with the dance teacher could thus serve as an assessment exercise as well as an important part of the whole collaborative learning toward which the project aimed. The lesson encouraged students to use time lines and maps in order to help the dance teacher isolate Timbuktu from out of a generalized and homogenized (and nonhistorical) Africa.

Finally, the unit involved a trip to the Yale University art museum to visit the West African galleries. This trip provided the opportunity to work out what museum-school collaboration might mean if full integration were to be the goal. My first step was always to visit the museum ahead of the student visit and to view what the students would be seeing, then to work out what connections could be made with the curriculum. Since the objects at Yale are nineteenth- and twentieth-century carvings from West Africa, the link had to be the period after the Moroccan conquest of Timbuktu and the centuries of European penetration and colonialism. What seemed most relevant about European colonialism in this context was the absence within European representations of Africa of any mention of the earlier empires, and in their place, the picture of the "dark continent." Missing from images of the dark continent is any sense of the lasting presence of Islam in the region, and instead, the image of traditional, village-based societies organized around kin groups and tribes. The image of the timeless village makes it much easier to present wood carvings as productions of traditional African society, changeless and timeless. In this idyllic setting the objects can easily be presented as manifestations of culture, without any necessary historical context.

As it happened, the Guggenheim Museum in New York was mounting its massive African show, "Art of a Continent," during the time when we were developing the curriculum. Articles in the catalogue, to be read by teachers, provided material for raising questions that students could address during and after their visit to the Yale University Gallery. I used excerpts from an article by Anthony Appiah to call attention to the European representation of Africa as the "Dark Continent" and the homogenizing of all sub-Saharan Africa, or, as Appiah calls it, the presentation of the whole as "a single continuum."[3] Appiah goes on to note that traditions of mask making and performance are different throughout the whole of the West African region. Art historian Susan Blier notes that today's Western audience for African art still finds it difficult to interpret West African masks as anything other than embodiments of traditional and timeless village Africa.

What we have, in the general American understanding of Africa that allows for the belief in timeless tradition, is an "erasure" of the history that the Timbuktu unit hoped to bring alive. The possible dangers in arts collaboration that pays no attention to current historical knowledge is that the very stereotypes that block the development of a non-Eurocentric sensibility can be reinforced.

Scholar Collaboration: San Juan, Puerto Rico's Capitol City

Although many people who are not professional historians feel very confident in their knowledge of the past, very few people actually know much about what history is for the practicing historian. Why there should be such a discrepancy we do not really know, but that there is was evident throughout the curriculum process. The very lack of difficulty that many in the project experienced over the inclusion of a supposed all-African dance in a unit on Timbuktu in the eleventh to the sixteenth centuries, or the inclusion of a dance celebrating Lord Krishna in a South Indian style in the unit on Banaras, was jarring in ways that pushed me toward becoming ever more picky about spelling out connections, no matter how tenuous. In the introduction to the "Cities" curriculum I had taken recourse in high abstraction and presented the "world" as the manifestation of interlinked historical narratives. That attempt issued from frustration over how to help teachers distinguish between a layperson's view of the past as something solid out there, and the historian's view of the past as constructed knowledge and interpretation.

Some of our scholar collaborators were more sensitive than others to the fact that many of our teachers were not undergraduate history majors and themselves needed help in moving from a grab-bag approach to the past in which anything you find is acceptable to some sense of how to frame an historically pertinent question. Those who were more sensitive to teachers' needs took great creative pains to elaborate a coherent historical context. And to my mind the most compelling of these efforts was manifested in the unit on San Juan.

The unit took shape from the posing of an historical problem that our scholar thought teachers and students could address: although San Juan, on the eastern coast of the island and the colonial capitol since 1507, was clearly to be the focus of the unit, the city of Ponce, on the southwestern coast, ought also to claim our attention since it had become the cultural capitol of the island in the nineteenth century and was the urban center from which had emerged the first steps toward claiming independence from Spain. What was the interplay between the two cities? What had happened in Ponce that failed to happen, or just did not happen in San Juan?

The challenge was to figure out how to turn what could be a rather dry and complicated story of economic and political change resulting from an intensification of international involvements in the eighteenth century into one that would engage teachers, and through them, their students. What our scholar did was to isolate an event in the middle of the eighteenth century that seemed able to bear the weight of serving as a watershed, a center point for a "before and after" organization of the material.

The pivotal event was a report commissioned by the government of Spain and submitted to the government in 1765 on the condition of the colony of Puerto Rico. Of all Spain's colonies in Latin America, Puerto Rico appeared to be the least prosperous, its imperial government in San Juan subsidized by Mexico, and its only value to the mother country being in its strategic location at the eastern end of the Caribbean.

Alesandro O'Reilly, an Irishman in the service of the Spanish crown, toured the island and issued his report. Puerto Rico was underpopulated and underdeveloped. Agriculture consisted mostly of subsistence farming and the population was made up of thieves, rascals, and ex-convicts. O'Reilly recommended a complete overhaul of the legal system, opening up the island to immigration of middle-class white Europeans willing to take up cash-crop agriculture in return for land in order to bring the island to a par with neighboring islands rich in the production of sugar cane and coffee. O'Reilly recommended the privatization of property, enclosure of public lands, and generous gifts of land to prospective plantation owners.

The responses to O'Reilly's report were dramatic. European immigrants did come to the island and were given land in the area around Ponce, where they developed a thriving sugar-cane-producing site. By the early nineteenth century the slave population of the island had increased as had the wealth of the plantation owners, and Ponce had become a cosmopolitan city with an orientation toward France and Britain rather than Spain. Tensions developed between rich and poor over demands for increased production, and repressive legislation was passed in response, favoring the rich. An intellectual elite emerged in Ponce, with connections to revolutionary groups abroad. Once known as Spain's most loyal colony, Puerto Rico by the mid-nineteenth century could boast an independence movement of its own. O'Reilly clearly had a lot to answer for: or did he? In 1765 he had sowed the seeds for prosperity, and a hundred years later the people had reaped revolution. Was it his fault? Here our scholar suggested that the O'Reilly report be used to raise questions about the intended and unintended consequences of actions. Students were to work through the materials presented and then, from their own situation as historical analysts, write a letter to O'Reilly reporting to him on the intended and unintended consequences of his action.

What I have just described was the final shaping to a unit over the six-year period of the project. What made the final coming together of the subject so exciting was that our scholar had stayed with the unit for the whole time, taking an interest in it, in the teachers who would be teaching it, and in the students who would be studying it. Part of his devotion to the San Juan unit in "Cities" came from his involvement as the consulting scholar in the other two curricula: "Becoming American" for fourth graders and "Migration" for fifth graders. On the subject of San Juan, and Puerto Rico in general, we had an opportunity to implement one of the guiding principles of the whole three-year curriculum, which was not to introduce a subject and then drop it. For example, I did not want to allow American Indians into the curriculum only to serve as the people who were on the shores, waiting for the Pilgrims and Puritans to arrive before they disappeared again, only to re-emerge as they start out on the Trail of Tears two hundred years later. Hence, I included paintings by contemporary American Indian painters, reflecting on their past, as I had done for West Africans. Students begin to learn about Puerto Rico in the introductory unit to the fourth-grade curriculum, when they can study images of Taino deities. They study Columbus' arrival and meeting with a Taino chief, Gayacanagari, and they meet Father Pane, who traveled with Columbus on his second voyage specifically to collect information on what the inhabitants of the newly discovered islands believed. They are exposed to archaeological knowledge that suggests how Tainos built their villages, what they ate, what games they played. Finally, people claiming Taino descent reemerge in the fifth-grade curriculum as part of Puerto Rico's migrant population in Hartford, the student's own city, asserting their cultural and historical identity.

Making It History: Edo into Tokyo

Tokyo was the last city the students studied, the last in the curriculum, and the last unit we put into final, written shape. Everything that we had learned in doing the other units informed the way we organized the Tokyo unit, and many of the interpretive threads we had introduced were finally woven together. The Tokyo unit has a strong narrative flow and is brimming over with gorgeous visual material. It was great fun to work on; many teachers have said it was good to teach; and teachers reported that students found the exploration of Tokyo's history stimulating.

As with the other units, the Tokyo unit went through several drafts. The first time around, it was a repository for what were becoming the standard signs of Japan in the elementary school multicultural curriculum: references to the tea ceremony and flower arranging, origami instructions, pictures of kimonos, and samurai stories. A few versions later, and thanks to our consulting scholar, it had become an exploration of what had been done by the government during the Tokugawa period that helped ensure the success of reforms undertaken by the Meiji reformers.

At the center of the lesson sequence is the arrival of the American, Admiral Perry, in (what became) Tokyo Bay in 1853. How were Japanese leaders to respond to this attempt by a foreign power to open up Japanese ports to foreign trade? We introduce material on the debates surrounding the decision to sign the "unequal treaties," and then on steps taken by the leaders to ensure that Japan would emerge as a country equal in strength and dignity to the countries of the West. The narrative includes the restoration of the emperor as Japan's ruler, and the end of Tokugawa rule; political, military, and educational reforms throughout the country; the decision to send Japanese abroad to gain knowledge and to bring in foreign experts to help build modern institutions; and Japan's success in defeating Russia in battle in 1905.

The narrative is tremendously enriched by moving backward in time to ask whether any steps taken by the Tokugawas, in fact, helped pave the way for the Meiji reformers. Here we go back to the establishment of Tokugawa rule in 1600, which brought several warring states, each led by its own *daimyo* (feudal lord) under one rule; the establishment of the new government in what had been a small fishing village, Edo (which under Meiji became Tokyo); and the decision of one of the early Tokugawas to rid the country of foreign (Portuguese) missionaries, outlaw Christianity, forbid Japanese to travel abroad, and close the country to foreigners.

The Japanese insularity that supposedly ensued from these actions of the early Tokugawas is sometimes offered as an explanation for why the Meiji reformers had to work so diligently to bring Japan into the modern age. Students studying "Cities" would be able to offer a much more nuanced explanation. Actually, The Tokugawa rulers did not completely close off the country. They allowed the Dutch, a major European power in the seventeenth century, to remain in a small section of Nagasaki, and to engage in trade. The continuous presence of the Dutch in Japan throughout the whole of the 250-year Tokugawa period served several purposes: it kept open Japanese access to trade; it made it possible for at least a small number of Japanese intellectuals to keep up with European scientific discoveries and advances in military technology; and it produced primary sources embodying a European view of events in Japan during the period.

Tokugawa rulers instituted a system of alternate attendance, according to which each daimyo, or once-independent feudal lord, had to spend every second year in Edo. During the year that he was in his own domain, he had to leave his family in residence in Edo. Daimyos traveled with retinues of thousands, so the roads were always full. The system of alternate attendance facilitated the change in Edo from small fishing village to perhaps the largest city in the world in the eighteenth century, with a population of over 1 million. Not only did the system help to centralize the country, an important step toward facilitating the work of the Meiji reformers centuries later, but it also spawned the growth of Japanese urban culture, particularly *kabuki* theater, *ukiyo-e* woodblock printing, and several schools of poetry.

Dutch residents in Nagasaki were required to pay their respects to the Tokugawa lord in Edo, and there are firsthand accounts by Dutch travelers of the crowded, major route from Kyoto to Edo. Daimyos with their *samurai* guards were always to be seen, either going to or coming from Edo. Gifts sent to the Tokugawa ruler were transported over this road, and there is even a record of an elephant, sent by the Chinese, making the trip.

The road from Kyoto to Tokyo was a channel for news of the outside world to flow into Japan. By no means, of course, were the Japanese as informed about European countries and America as they were to become after 1853; but neither were they totally ignorant. There were many, especially in the samurai class, who had labored mightily to keep up with events in Europe by learning Dutch. The major task before them, in 1853, was to abandon Dutch and learn English, and as they did so, they discovered that they were not so ignorant of the workings of European technology as they feared. There is one story of a group of Japanese visitors to America in the 1880s who are shown a sugar-refining factory, with their American guests assuming they will be amazed. They knew about the process of refining, having read about it in Dutch works and committed the process to memory; what was more surprising, one writer said, was American waste.

There is rich documentation for the Tokugawa and Meiji periods, and students studying "Cities" have ample opportunity to work with primary sources as they become familiar with the narrative being unfolded. There are also fabulous visual materials. The road between Kyoto and Tokyo, over which so many daimyo, samurai, and foreign visitors traveled to pay their respects to the Tokugawa ruler, is the famous Tokaido Road, illustrated by the artist Hiroshige.

The Tokyo unit focuses attention on what the Meiji reformers had to work with in order to transform Japan into the country they intended it to be. It raises a legitimate question of historical inquiry, and it proceeds to construct an explanatory narrative through which the question can be addressed. Through its attention to the American connection, the unit also draws upon interpretations used in other units. Japan, of course, was not an official colony of any Western country. Through the decisions to send many young Japanese on research trips to the United States and Europe and to hire hundreds of American and European advisors to work in education at all levels, build buildings, provide industrial know-how, shape political ideas, and the like, the Meiji reformers opened the country to Western cultural influence. In shaping the final sequence of lessons, I was attentive to ways in which scholarly approaches to the study of cultural influence in colonial situations could provide insights for understanding what was happening in Tokyo.

What makes the Tokyo unit stand out more than the others in my mind, though, is the great good luck we had in working with arts and museum collaborators. Each unit after the first one begins with a bridge lesson, linking the city just studied to the one about to be studied. Some of the links stretched the imagination. To get from Hartford in the twentieth century to Athens 2,500 years earlier, we had students assume the role of time travelers. Some of these linkages were more plausible, as when the time travelers returned to Hartford at the end of the Athens unit and prepared to go on a pilgrimage to Banaras. We had to forge a link between San Juan and Tokyo, and we found the means to do so in one of our local house museums. The Butler-McCook House in Hartford was the residence of a family, some of whose members on the McCook side had fought in the Spanish American War. One of the Butler-McCook sisters had gone to China at the turn of the century to be a missionary, and in 1908, her father, Reverend McCook, took his other daughter on a trip to visit the sister, with a lengthy stopover in Japan. McCook was a good tourist. He kept a detailed diary, available in the house museum today, describing what he did, where he went, what he saw, with whom he visited, and what he bought. The house is full of his Japanese memorabilia, including bronze vessels, porcelain vases, and dinnerware, and a large collection of samurai armor, helmets, and sword hilts. Once he got home, McCook continued to record the Japanese objects that he bought from dealers in Hartford. All this was material for the beginning of the unit.

McCook was a conscientious but modest collector since he was not a man of means. Not far from where he lived in Hartford was the house of the Sam and Elizabeth Colt, he the inventor of the Colt revolver, and she a more sophisticated collector. Elizabeth's entire collection, including the Japanese items that appealed to her, was donated to the Athenaeum. The collection includes two large porcelain vases she bought from the Japanese pavilion at the Philadelphia World's Fair of 1875. During the time when we were developing the curriculum it was our great good fortune to be able to take the students to a show at the Athenaeum featuring Elizabeth Colt's collection.

The curator of the Elizabeth Colt show had mounted a show not too long before titled "The Japanese Idea." The exhibition explored the craze for things Japanese that had swept American cities after Perry's visit in 1853. Much of the material from the catalogue could be incorporated into the curriculum to help students explore the question of what Americans knew about Japan a hundred years ago.

Finally, within the region is the house of the Pope family, collectors of Impressionist painters in the 1880s and 1890s, and of Japanese woodblock prints as they became available on the Paris market. Students toured the house as part of the curriculum, and the Tokyo unit includes reproductions from the collection.

So rich was this material that we used it to develop lessons in addition to the bridge lesson featuring the Fighting McCooks, who fought in the Spanish American War, and their nephew, Reverend McCook, who traveled to Japan on his way to China. The visual and textual resources from these three sites enabled us to trace American interest in Japan from the time of Admiral Perry's arrival through the early decades of the twentieth century. We could include lessons designed to conjure up the excitement of the World's Fair, when Hartford provided a train direct from the city to the fairgrounds in Philadelphia and where Elizabeth Colt bought her Japanese vases; the enthusiasm of the Pope family for woodblock prints, including some of Hiroshige's views of the Tokaido Road; and finally, Reverend McCook's interest in samurai armor.

Conclusion

What should be the shape and content of a world history course for sixth graders? When our students went on their museum trips in connection with the units they proudly sported their buttons, "We're Making History." For some, these school trips were their first visits to any museums, and for others, they were the first visits to some of the sites. We were making history in the sense that we were including visits to, and work in, these sites as part of what the students were studying.

Project collaborators were making history in another sense as well. There were no models for tying together these six cities in the ways that we had done. There were no interpretive grids already existing that we superimposed over all the cities, and no uniform conclusions. At the end, we had a curriculum that was uniquely our own, the work of our three hundred collaborators. It was like no other curriculum in world history. It embodied our best efforts, and it was our responsibility.

As we proceeded, we defined the role of the scholar in projects such as this as involving much more than enrichment of the teachers' content base. Scholars participated in the sequential shaping of lessons, ensuring that the curriculum had a firm historical orientation. My role, as it had developed, was to coordinate the various scholarly contributions and to keep open communication among all the collaborators. By the time we were working on the second draft of the curriculum, I developed a pattern. I met with the scholar consultant for the first unit and described the whole curriculum and our objectives for it, particularly our desire that it embody recent scholarship on the area in which the city under study was located. We talked about possibilities for developing the unit and I left with a reading list that would familiarize me with some of the ways in which that particular city had been studied.

At the next series of meetings I brought together the consulting scholar and the teachers and all of us then worked out a lesson sequence. In later meetings I worked with the teachers and other educational consultants to refine the lessons and work out assessments.

When we were working with museums, I went first to study what students would be seeing, then, using scholarly sources on museum practice and the exhibiting and understanding of objects from outside the West, I worked up outlines for lessons that would integrate the visual materials into what the students were learning. I then worked with the museum educators who would be training the docents, telling them what the unit was about, what the whole curriculum was about, and how I thought we could structure the museum visit. Where possible, we all then met together with the teachers to produce the final version of the museum lesson and a follow-up lesson for the classroom.

This was labor-intensive work. Even more than scholarship on the cities to which I was directed by the consulting scholars, I gained a sense of what Eurocentric meant in relation to visual objects and museum practice. Objects from ancient classical civilizations, the Chola bronzes from India, for instance, stand in our museums as art, as do masks from West Africa, but it is art with a difference. Unlike Greek vases, which we are encouraged to admire and appreciate for their formal qualities, objects from outside Europe and America are supposed to inform us about the culture which produced them. Often this means little more than to be able to identify a many-armed deity as Indian. I am oversimplifying, but such interpretations have dominated in our museums.

If being Eurocentric means, in some senses, seeing Europe as the place where art is created, and the rest of the world as the place where objects embody culture, then being non-Eurocentric must mean seeing something else, seeing in different ways. Although it may have appeared contrived, to insist that students leave Banaras and make a trip to the capitol of the Chola Empire in order to see the famous Siva Nataraj, I meant it to make the important point that this image did have an inventor. If the precise artist is not known, the workshop in which the image was produced is known, and so is the name of the royal patron. The creation of the image can be precisely dated. There is a good deal more to say about the object than that it is Indian.

Until recently, our museums and galleries paid no attention to contemporary art production in other places. Technically, we could call the process a form of erasure, a denial that there is contemporary art production or that it could be of any importance or interest to us. By bringing in the work of contemporary African painters to the Timbuktu unit, I had hoped to call attention to the fact that there were African painters working today, and that we could look at their work as a means to see how these painters were reflecting on their pasts.

I am convinced that contemporary scholarship has much to tell us about how we might learn to see beyond the contours of a Eurocentric frame. The question, of course, is what scholarship, and how we are to master enough of it to make it accessible to students at all levels of our educational system. Our scholars were specialists in their regions; those who studied areas other than Europe and the United States had been trained under the rubric of area studies. Because of the duration of the project, the fact that the curriculum went through many revisions, and the procedures I had worked out for communicating among collaborators, it was possible to build a behind-the-scenes frame of conceptualization for the project as a whole, which at a deep level, made the curriculum make sense. That frame was decidedly interdisciplinary, bringing together history, anthropology, literary study, and the emerging field of cultural and postcolonial studies. At the center of the frame was a question: how do we understand Eurocentrism in ways that will enable us to see beyond it? To put it another way, we have been looking through the Eurocentric frame for a long time; how long will it take to disassemble that frame so that we can see in new ways?

Notes

1. The project, titled the Connecticut Humanities Alliance and part of a nationwide project of the Rockefeller Foundation titled CHART (Collaborations in Humanities and Arts), was a systemwide endeavor involving teachers and students in grades 4, 5, and 6 in Hartford area schools. The lifetime of the project in Hartford was from 1990 to 1997. Information on the three curricula in American and World History can be obtained from the Connecticut Humanities Council, Middletown, CT.

2. Diana L. Eck, *Banaras, City of Light* (Princeton, NJ: Princeton University Press, 1982).

3. Kwame Anthony Appiah, "Why Africa, Why Art?" *Africa: The Art of the Continent* (New York: Guggenheim Museum, n.d.), pp. 5–8.

3

The World After Columbus
Learning a Lot About a Little

MARK WILLIAMS

If you are able to make a list of everything in the history of the world that young people should understand, *and then* figure out a way to fit all of that into one curriculum, you have my undying admiration. Over the past two decades there have been a few attempts to accomplish the first of those noble aspirations, but the authors of the various history and social studies content standards have so far neglected to consider the second.[1]

It may be impossible. The acrimonious debates over the ideological implications of differing sets of standards suggest that teachers will always face complaints unless they present all sides of historical issues and develop lessons on the heroes of every interest group and nationality. That aside, each set of standards as written calls for the coverage of a body of content so voluminous that not even the most coordinated school system could teach it all in thirteen years of schooling—even if its curriculum leaders could count on students remaining in their district from kindergarten through high school.

I have long since given up on the everything-they-should-know-about approach. I teach world history, but only a small slice of it. Some will say my high school students miss out on a lot—that in a year at that point in their lives, they could learn about so much more; but at least I can say that the small terrain they traverse on the vast landscape of world history is terrain they will know well. And in knowing it well, I think they find it more interesting, which is the ultimate objective. Once they love history, then there is actually a chance they might learn a significant share of all that the "experts" think they should know.

For my small slice, I have selected the period of time from 1492 to about 1750. That's right. "The World After Columbus" is a yearlong world history course that, for the first time in the history of the world, covers fewer years than a typical United States history course! And why shouldn't that be the case? World history is, after all, about more than one nation. This is the description of the course as it appears in our school catalogue: "1492 was a watershed year, not only for European civilization, but for all peoples of the world. Land travelers and mariners from all over the world had been part of trade networks prior to this date, but after Columbus, the whole world would be connected through overseas expansion, as nations competed for wealth and power beyond their shores. This course examines world history between 1492 and 1750. In investigating case studies of encounter, interaction, and change in Africa, the Americas, and Asia, as well as in Europe, students learn about the emergence of new world systems, where some Europeans may have dominated politically, but were never in control of the vast changes taking place among peoples of other continents, nor even among themselves. Also, to understand the roots of these changes, as well as their implications for the future and the world in which we live today, students look back from this watershed period of European expansion as well as forward into the modern world."

So, actually, it *is* a little more ambitious than its dates sound. There is the forward- and backward-looking dimension of it. And there are grander aspirations as well.

As this course description suggests, the content of the course actually forms a narrative of cultural encounter and change. Reaching beyond the traditional Eurocentric story of explorers and colonizers, this narrative involves the actions of Asian, African, and American peoples, as well as people of all continents who were not among the powerful and wealthy. At a deeper level it asks students to come to some understanding of how power and wealth are a part of human experience, of the varieties of encounter among different peoples (trade and learning as well as conflict), and of the ways in which human beings adapt to change. Although there is considerable time spent on case studies involving English people and encounters in what became an Atlantic system dominated by English law and mercantilism, students learn about all of this in a global context that encourages them to look at the growth of the English empire from many perspectives. Ultimately, the course amounts to an *introduction* rather than a comprehensive examination. The idea is not to provide information on *everything* young people need to know, but to *open their eyes* to all of the possibilities of trends, events, people, and perspectives that one should study in order to come to an understanding of how the world developed the way it did—how we, the human race, got to be the way we are.

The assumption, then, is that with this course, we are making a beginning, and that students are expected to continue in a lifelong learning process about the world and its people. Of course, they must have the intellectual tools to do that, and so, thinking processes are central to the curriculum. These "thinking processes" include those that are defined in the *National Standards for History*, and have been central to the thinking of process-oriented educators for decades.[2] The course is designed purposefully to teach young people about the discipline of history. Students are taught to ask questions the way historians ask them, to look at the kinds of sources that historians look at, to use analytical and interpretive tools employed by historians, and generally to appreciate the importance of curiosity and creativity in studying the past.

Finally, in teaching this course, I devote significant time and energy toward motivational goals. If I am to develop lifetime learners I need to make the course fun and exciting. The selected time period certainly helps toward that end. With all the twists and turns of politics and cultural interaction, there are no dull moments, and there is much happening that young people will naturally want explained. Even so, I keep textbooks as far away from class as possible—the students work together to do their own explaining. I also inject a good deal of local history into the mix, and that has the advantage of illustrations coming to life in the students' own backyard. We play games, reenact negotiations and debates, watch feature films (as with textbooks, though, I avoid documentaries), rustle through old documents as though we were in search of ancient treasure, and visit local museums and other historic sites. Children learn and learn to learn by playing, and in this course we play around a lot.

What follows is a detailed outline of the course. At The Loomis Chaffee School, our academic year is divided into trimesters. Hence the tripartite division of the course. Some of the teaching strategies referred to in this outline will be discussed in greater depth in Chapter 6. (Note: Throughout the year students collect articles from the *New York Times* that relate to the events that we study, and write a reflection on each explaining the relationship of the article to the historic events.)

Part I: Old Worlds Make New Connections, 1492–1600

Introduction: What Is History?

In this section of the course students find out about the kinds of events they will be studying, as well as the nature of thinking historically. From the start, I want to stimulate and encourage them to ask questions, which will give them a sense of directing the investigation of that history to some extent themselves. It is important to develop habits of curiosity early in the course and to begin to train students to welcome their curiosity about the past and to articulate it in the form of historical questions, questions pivoting on the three great historical questions: what happened, why did it happen, and what does it mean?

Focal Issues

1. What is history and what do historians do? What does it mean to "think historically"?

2. What is the subject matter of world history between 1492 and 1750, and, more specifically, between 1492 and 1600?

3. What do we want to know about that time period?

We begin with a short "admission test" in which students answer, as well as they can, questions about the period of world history between 1492 and 1750 (referred to in the *National Standards for History* as Era 6 for World History and Eras 1 and 2 for United States History[3]). This little questionnaire gives me some information about what they know, or don't know, and about how they express themselves. Students also write about the history they have studied in the past and what they think history is all about. From there, through the medium of a folktale ("The Wonderful Tar Baby Story"), we move into some initial thinking about the nature of history. The story is one told by a former slave and contains echoes of the African past. The telling of it provides illustrations for thoughts about storytelling, cultural identity, human nature, and adaptation during a time of great change. Simply by thinking about these matters students will start to understand the complexity of history and its subject matter.

Next we will have students actually *do* history by working with some source material on the "Lost Colony" of Roanoak. The English experience at Roanoak in the 1580s is a superb beginning because it not only presents a ready-made mystery which will provoke historical inquiry about the event itself, but on another level, is suggestive of many of the elements of European expansion, succeeding interaction among different peoples, and processes of change which emerged in the world after 1492. First we have students read some background about Walter Raleigh's project to establish an English outpost in North America. Students then learn about the failure of the first effort and the mysterious disappearance of the second colony. Its governor, John White, who had returned to England to gather supplies, was delayed three years because of the attempted invasion of England by Spain (the Battle of the Spanish Armada) in 1588. When he finally returned in 1590 he found traces of the little outpost, but none of his "planters." Immediately the students ask what happened to the "Lost Colony"?

This question leads to some investigation of primary sources: John White's drawings of the Roanoak people made on the exploratory voyage in 1584, some maps of the area made by the English explorers, and excerpts from White's journal describing interaction between the English and the Roanoaks and what he found on his return in 1590. Students work in small groups developing theories based on the evidence in these sources, present their ideas in a general discussion, and then write a short paper defending their theory about what happened to the colonists.[4] The paper is diagnostic. That is, it gives me a sense of each student's writing skills in the beginning of the year, and after I have returned the papers with comments, it gives students an idea of expectations for future written work. Since no one really knows what happened to the colonists, it is not important for students to get the "right" answer, and it should become apparent to them that the emphasis here is on developing a "reasonable" answer, given the clues in the sources.

The students then watch the three-hour PBS production of *Roanoak*, which ends with the mystery still unsolved, but, along the way, depicts in wrenching depth the interaction that took place between the Roanoaks and the English and serves as a good example of historical interpretation. While they are watching it in school, students can do some free reflection on their own, writing journal entries and responding in writing to journal entries of other students. I will encourage students to understand that the movie is an interpretation—that it is the work of historians and film producers, and not necessarily the way things really happened. Students also spend some time on some background reading on the Battle of the Spanish Armada, which battle they will reenact in a simulation board game when the movie is over (see Figure 3–1). Doing the reading assignment gives them a chance to begin practicing sound study and notetaking techniques, and I will collect their reflections and their first set of reading notes for comment at this point.

The movie and the game, together with the Roanoak exercise, should provoke of a lot of questions, and I try to help them to organize the questions into a framework something like: (1) questions about *forces behind* European expansion in the sixteenth century (both European and hemispheric roots); (2) questions about the particulars of *what happened* during that century as European explorers, traders, soldiers, adventurers, missionaries, and opportunists met and interacted with people all over the world; and (3) questions about the *political dynamics of sixteenth-century Europe,* which played an important role in shaping the processes of change that developed throughout the world after 1492, and which also give hints about how the European

Figure 3–1. *"World After Columbus" students fighting the battle of the Spanish Armada*

discovery of the Americas and sea routes to Asia were changing Europe in many ways. This is essentially the framework of investigation for the first part of the course. Other questions might look forward to the impact of patterns of interaction on the future of societies about the world, and raise the possibility of relationships with issues that occupy the world community today. At this point, students will be encouraged to develop a habit of searching through a good news source (the *New York Times* is ideal) for articles that seem to echo the trends and developments we are studying and to keep a file of them for reflection and discussion.

Overall, the introduction sets the tone for the course. I get to know the students and the point at which they begin in terms of their previous knowledge of the subject, and in terms of their thinking and writing skills. They get a taste of the course as not only a study of European expansion, multicultural interaction, and the global changes that resulted, but also one in which they, the students, take on considerable responsibility for their own learning, and in the process *learn to learn*. They should begin to see that the standard routines of the class (small-group work, individual reflection on the topics, inquiry-oriented study on intriguing and challenging issues, sound study habits involving a good deal of writing, and materials and activities that are fun and bring history to life) directly reinforce the concept of a student-centered course of study and reflect what historical thinking involves. These revelations should show up in their group discussions and in their last notebook reflections on the classes in which we discuss the big questions of the course. Now they are ready to begin some investigation into forces behind European expansion.

Thus, for an overall assessment of how well I have introduced the course I use:

1. admissions test (prior knowledge, attitudes, skills—for diagnostic purposes)
2. essay on Roanoak (prior skills—for diagnostic purposes)
3. degree of enthusiasm in class activities
4. notebooks: organization, secondary source notes, reflections on *Roanoak*, the Armada, and focal issues of the course
5. class discussion—quality of questions raised on the final day

Investigation No. 1: The World on the Eve of European Expansion

Focal Issues

1. Why did Europeans begin searching for sea routes to other continents in the fifteenth century (and not before)?
2. What made it possible for them to succeed?
3. Why didn't people of other continents "discover" Europe?

As with most of the topics of this course, there is no way that students will become experts, or know all there is to know about the subject at hand in a few weeks' time. We will rely upon historians to provide important information and interpretation, but in a subject of this scope the danger of doing that alone is that the history will lose its connection with real life and become too abstract to be either useful or interesting. Thus, the dilemma: the broad trends must have flesh and blood, but in a short amount of time we also want the students to come away with meaningful and well-founded historical understanding. The resolution of the dilemma lies in breaking up the investigation among groups of students, and then training students to condense what they have learned and share it with each other.

First I will announce that, for their "test" on the upcoming unit of study, students will be asked to critique a textbook selection about the forces behind European expansion. The text selection, by G. Edmund Mythmaker (alias me), presents a traditional Eurocentric version of the beginnings of expansion, and has a number of errors, both trivial and interpretive, which we hope the students will recognize after their investigation is done. It is also a parody of boring textbook writing. They will be writing a memo to their employer about whether the book should be published, and then rewrite the narrative as it should be written, recognizing, it is hoped, the importance of taking a broader perspective, of understanding the complexity of historical forcces, and of writing engaging narrative. They will have, from the beginning, a list of standards that the written work should meet. In addition they will get a list of standards for a group presentation.

For reading material I have made selections from the following sources. The published material is held on reserve in our library, and my own introductory writings and documentary materials are duplicated for each student.

- *The Discoverers,* by Daniel Boorstin, Chapters 15–19, 26, 61–63 (discusses topics such as the Mongolian Empire and overland trade networks, the conflicts over control of Southwest Asia, contacts between Europeans and the Islamic Empire in Africa, technological developments in Asia, Africa, and Europe—in printing, writing, mapmaking, and navigation—and Chinese and Portuguese mariners)
- Lynda Shaffer, "Hemispheric Roots of Columbian Voyages" (discusses non-Western origins of navigational and sailing technology used for European exploration)
- *Through African Eyes,* pp. 21–79 (discusses African empires of Ghana, Mali, and Songhay, and African trade routes)
- Jackdaw packets on the Inquisition and Islam (contain facsimiles of primary sources as well as secondary source readings)
- "Religion and Government" handout (my own introduction to Christianity in Medieval Europe)
- "Early Church Doctrine" document collection (contains excerpts from Augustine, Aquinas, Durand, Boniface VIII, Goliard Poets, John of Salisbury)

As stated above, the reading material is parceled out among groups of students. I divide the above readings into the following group topics:

1. The Judaeo-Christian Tradition
2. Overland Trade Before 1492
3. Technology for Sailing the Oceans
4. The Great African Empires
5. The Islamic Empire

Each topic has assigned readings and some written guidelines for discussion and thought. The group may split some of the readings up, or have all read everything. After a few days of work and discussion, the members of each group should plan a presentation of what they have learned. This may take any number of forms: panel discussion, skit, role play, written handouts, display, etc. Presentations should be accompanied by questions from the other students and general discussion. The written memo and textbook section, as well as frequent notebook checks, round out the assessment.

Of course, any historian will note that there will be considerable overlap among these topics, and one major objective here, in fact, should be to have students realize that, before 1492, the world itself was, indeed, very much interconnected—at least each hemisphere was within itself. Without this vast web of contacts through trade, war, and exchange of knowledge, there would have been no expansion of Europe. In the next investigation we will see how these connections were necessary for exploration, trade, and conquest. One connecting link among all of the topics themselves will be geography. It is essential, early in the course, for students to develop a good sense of location and place and to begin to think about the relationship between climate and topography and the way people live. We will do some serious map work (with outline maps) in this regard. At the conclusion of the investigation we will have identified a number of places that have figured into our studies and that students will be able to locate on the world map. Among these will be major mountain ranges, desert areas, bodies of water, climatic zones, and rivers. These should show up in their narratives.

I expect that notebooks will contain important information, and that in many ways students will demonstrate that they have thought seriously about how all the information fits together in a story. The main components of the story revolve around the importance of trade, religion, learning, technology, and the shifting of empires in "setting up" Europe for a period of expansion beginning in the late fifteenth century. It is very important that students show, in their group discussions and presentations, in their reflections, and in their papers that they understand both the multiplicity of these factors as well as the many different peoples and places that must be taken into account. The opening of direct trade routes between Europe and China by the expansion of the Tartar Khans in the thirteenth century was important, for example, particularly when we consider the effect of the closing of those routes in the fourteenth century by an Islamic power. Was the struggle between the Christian world and the Islamic Empire a struggle between competing religions, or a struggle for control of wealth? We should see students actively engaged in thinking such as this. Again, we can hardly expect them to become experts, but the effort to create a coherent narrative should be made by each of them, and even if the narrative is incomplete and, in the end, not as coherent as we might like, it should be reasonable and more sophisticated than their answers on the admission test of the first day. Evidence that they are having some fun and are intrigued by the subject is even more important, since it would suggest that they might return to these issues sometime in their future studies.

While papers are being written, and rewritten after my comments, students will watch the movie *Christopher Columbus: The Discovery*. This is an interesting character study and adventure movie that raises a lot of good questions for thought and leads well into the next investigation.

Investigation No. 2: Encounters, Changes, and Conquests

Now that students are aware of encounters among people of the Eastern Hemisphere before 1492, they will learn about the encounters which ensued as Portugal and Spain began the search for sea routes to "the East." Here we carry over the understanding that encounter does not necessarily take the form of conflict, but, in fact, has more often involved trade or learning, with conflict coming later, if at all, in a relationship. Students might begin to wonder what factors allow an encounter to proceed peacefully. There are certainly many cases in this investigation upon which to develop thoughts about the nature of encounter. As Spanish and Portuguese "adventurers" went their opposite ways in search of trade, gold, converts, and conquest, the people they met made varying decisions about the proper course of action to take in light of the newcomers to their world. In most cases the European arrival amounted to little more than a blip on a vast screen of local concerns, but sometimes, as in the case of the Aztecs, events developed quickly and permanently. In all cases the desire for power and wealth on both sides, as well as fear and distrust, played leading roles in the unfolding of the encounters.

Focal Issues

1. What happened when Europeans encountered people of other continents?
2. Was what happened inevitable, or were there other possible outcomes?

The plan for this investigation is basically the same as the first. While the students are working in groups, I try to take time out to work individually with students on their papers, preparing them for submission to the instructor. The written assessment at the end is a paper on whether or not our school should celebrate Columbus Day (Loomis Chaffee does not). They will address the paper to the student council.

Readings

- *Inter Caetera* (the papal bull dividing the New World between Spain and Portugal, 1493)—they all read this, with accompanying instructions on reading primary sources; and all receive maps of the world with "voyages of discovery" marked, and maps of the Americas to fill in.

- Daniel Boorstin, *The Discoverers,* Chapters 22 and 23 (on the Portuguese efforts to get to the Indian Ocean)
- document selections from accounts by Bartolomeu Dias, Vasco da Gama, Correa, de Camoens, Barbosa, Columbus, Vespucci, Páne, de Leon, Díaz del Castillo, Leon-Portilla, de Céspedes, Antonio de Espejo, Juan de Montoya, de Coronado, de Oviedo, de Xerxes, Juan Ginés de Sepúlveda and Bartolomé de Las Casas, Leo Africanus, Queen Isabella
- *The Broken Spears* (the Aztec accounts of Cortés' conquest of Mexico)
- Philip D. Curtin, *The Atlantic Slave Trade,* pp. 15–25, 95–116
- Michael Crowder, *West Africa,* pp. 47–64
- "Pizzaro," an article from *National Geographic* (February 1992)

Group Topics

1. The Real Indians Meet the Portuguese
2. Encounters in the Caribbean and Mexico
3. Encounters on the Mainland
4. Beginnings of the Atlantic Slave Trade

Again, we will emphasize the importance of knowledge of location and place; again, the students develop presentations from their materials; and students are encouraged to raise questions. When they are finished they write their persuasive paper on Columbus Day.

Students should see that there were many possibilities for outcomes, but that it was very difficult for those involved in each encounter to see "the big picture." The players were most interested in their own local and immediate concerns—the need to get further funding for more voyages, for example, influenced the manner in which Columbus behaved toward his "hosts." Moctezuma's obsession with his own power and past prophecies made it difficult for him to assess properly the strength of the invaders or devise appropriate strategies for defeating them. I hope to impress upon students that the notion that the Europeans were "more advanced" than other people around the earth is a myth, and that their success in conquest had more to do with playing their adversaries off each other, creating an atmosphere of fear, or with the spread of disease, than anything else. Finally, students should see here the beginnings of "the great exchange," much of it unanticipated, of plants, animals, minerals, ideas, people, and diseases and all of the consequences of that exchange. The notion that so much of what happened was unanticipated is something to which they should give serious thought.

Investigation No. 3: European Politics in the Sixteenth Century: Case Studies in the Emergence of Nation-States

While there is a tendency in this section to become somewhat "Anglocentric," it is important to investigate how England moved from a minor island kingdom to a major player in the struggle for world empire. This transition offers a case study in the internal politics of Europe as well as in the effects of overseas expansion on the lives of Europeans. The foundations for the transition from island to superpower were laid in the late sixteenth century as the country's leaders dealt with internal divisions in a manner that permitted and encouraged entry into the world economic system. This system was emerging as a result of the earlier interaction between the Spanish and Portuguese with peoples of Asia, Africa, and the Americas.

Focal Issues

1. How did overseas expansion and encounter with other peoples affect Europe?
2. In turn, how did the dynamics of European politics affect the continuing course of European expansion?

The plan is similar to the first two investigations. Students begin by reading "Henry VIII, the Great Divorce and Politics as Usual in Unusual Times" (a background piece I wrote) and then view the film *Anne of the Thousand Days*. We then move into raising questions, hypothesizing, and engaging in group study of various aspects of the politics of Europe in the late sixteenth century (I give them a series of charts showing the family trees of royal families of western Europe in the sixteenth century for reference).

Group Topics with Readings

1. Elizabeth I's Religious Policy: Conflict and Compromise
"From Subject to Citizen," readings on Edmund Campion, John Penry, and William Strickland, dissenters during the reign of Elizabeth I; evidence cards for a mock trial of Edmund Campion, Jesuit priest (they perform this trial as part of their presentation); Jackdaw packets: Henry VIII and His Six Wives, Martin Luther and Elizabeth I

2. Succession and Gender in Politics: France, Scotland, and England
"From Subject to Citizen" readings on Mary, Queen of Scots' execution, including letters by her son James VI of Scotland, Mary herself, Elizabeth, prime minister William Cecil, spymaster Francis Walsingham, and Elizabeth's secretary, William Davison; Jackdaw packet, "Mary, Queen of Scots"; film, *Mary, Queen of Scots* (the group views this on their own); documents giving evidence of attitudes toward women and women rulers; Jackdaw packet, "Elizabeth I"

3. Explorers, Merchants, and Sea Dogs—England Versus Spain
"From Subject to Citizen" readings on Drake, Hawkins, Jenkinson, and Frobischer with accompanying prospecti of their voyages; Jackdaw packet, "Francis Drake and the Golden Hind"

4. Religious Wars on the Continent: France and the Netherlands
Documents detailing France's politics in the sixteenth century, especially the wars of religion; material on the emergence of the Dutch Parliament and merchant class.

Intertwined in all of these topics is consideration of the sticky issue of the balance of power between the English Parliament and the monarch's prerogative, the unfolding of the Protestant Reformation, and the story of increasing consolidation of power on the part of European crowned heads of state. It is important to understand all of these issues not only as the institutional backdrop for the later "innovations" in the United States, but also to help understand the sense of superiority that accompanied Europeans as they expanded into other lands. The significant number of women who played leading roles in the politics of the time (Elizabeth I, Mary Tudor, Mary of Guise, Mary, Queen of Scots, Catherine de Medici, to name five quite prominent ones) also raises questions about the cultural backdrop of European expansion. As students come full circle to the eve of war between Spain and England they should have some sense of the role played by the Protestant and Catholic Reformations, national consolidation, and the resulting political struggles in affecting the course of European expansion. They should also begin to see that the European discovery of the Americas and of sea routes to Asia, and, in particular, the knowledge and products (especially gold and silver) that came from other lands, had a dramatic effect upon the course of European history. Next term we will continue investigation into the dynamics of Europe as expansion continued, but also we will see more clearly how the peoples of other continents played as important a role in all that was happening throughout the world.

For assessment purposes for this unit and for the entire first part of the course, I collect notebooks at this point, and assign a couple of essays (one asking students to summarize the group presentations and to discuss the impact of the voyages of discovery on European politics; and another that asks students to revisit one of their earlier writings and to revise and develop it with greater sophistication). It is important for students to demonstrate knowledge of major forces behind European expansion, including those forces that had their origins in other continents, the character of the diverse encounters which occurred as Europeans traveled around the world, the role played by European politics in the sixteenth century in shaping the activities of Europeans throughout the world, and, in turn, the effects of expansion and encounter with other peoples on European politics. On the surface, this structure may seem Eurocentric, and, indeed, the actions of Europeans are the focal points around which the investigations have moved. However, within each investigation, students will have been encouraged to see developments through the eyes of the Asians, Africans, and Americans and to understand how all of these people "made things happen." The outcome was usually disastrous for non-Europeans, and the world was surely reshaped to the advantage of Europeans (or, at least some Europeans), but that final outcome and shape just as surely had the imprint of actively participating peoples of all continents. We may bemoan what was lost and what the Europeans failed to appreciate in their fellow human beings, and we may condemn the attitudes, values, and structures among Europeans that contributed to those losses, but we need to go beyond that alone to understand what happened and the full effect of the outcomes of the encounters. In doing that we come to see the peoples of the other continents as human also, rather than "noble savages" or passive victims.

Part II: New Worlds, 1600–1688

Introduction: History and Ordinary People

Focal Issues

1. What was life like for ordinary Europeans in the late sixteenth and early seventeenth centuries?
2. How were ordinary people of Europe affected by the expansion of Europe into other continents, and to what extent were they involved in that expansion?

The war between England and Spain, which began in 1588, was a turning point for Europe and the world. Competition for power had been heating up for a long time, and exploded with the Battle of the Spanish Armada. The

Spanish defeat in the English Channel did not mean the end of the war, but it did signal the beginning of a new type of naval warfare, and the beginning of rivalry for world domination between nation-states who had been consolidating their power within Europe for some time. The century-old agreement between Spain and Portugal soon became irrelevant as first English and then Dutch and French ships sailed forth looking for opportunities of their own in the old "domains" of the Iberian powers. But was this surge in seafaring an expansion that involved all of the people of these countries? Or are we documenting only the activities of crowned heads of state and the merchants and mariners they sponsored? We already know that in England significant numbers of merchants and members of the landed gentry were becoming involved by investing in the enterprises the Queen could not afford to sponsor on her own. But what of ordinary people? How involved was the majority of the European population in these events that would reshape the whole world? Is it fair to say this was a "European" expansion? Was it the "coming of the white man?" Or were only a small number of white men involved?

We begin this part of the course with a look at the world of ordinary people in Europe. We first study the changing economy of the late sixteenth century through the game "People, Prices, and Products." By acting out the parts of tenant farmers, artisans, merchants, yeomen, landless laborers, and a few members of the upper class, students get a sense of how people made a living in early modern Europe and how the population explosion created a "price revolution" that affected everyone (see Figure 3–2). (For a more complete description of this game, see Chapter 6.) To help the students visualize this world we watch the movie *The Return of Martin Guerre,* and read one of

Figure 3–2. *"World After Columbus" students negotiating rents in "People, Prices, and Products"*

the "Reynard the Fox" stories. All of this is designed not only to get students to understand the world in which most Europeans lived, but also to encourage them to ask questions about the relationships among the classes, the effect of vast economic changes, the role of folk traditions in these relationships and changes, and the tension between the echoes of the "old religion" and the Christian worldview. They should see that, indeed, the big economic and political crises did involve the common people and had a lot to do with the attitudes of Europeans in general toward the rest of the world. This term will focus largely on Europe in crisis in the seventeenth century. As we study the various crises we will look at case studies of European expansion into various parts of the world, particularly English outposts in North America, and see how those crises affected the way Europeans attempted to establish "new worlds" where they could. A look at the ideas of Richard Hakluyt, an Elizabethan promoter of colonization, and consideration of how they relate to what we have learned about European society, will help the students to study these relationships in greater detail.

Investigation No. 1: An English Gentleman Decides: England in Crisis, 1600–1640

Here we begin to use England's expansion into North America as a case study in European colonialism. It should be noted that many American students study the colonial period in United States history over and over, and thus, it may be more appropriate to look at English expansion into other areas, or the expansion of another European nation into the New World, Asia, or Africa as a case study of colonialism. However, because the materials that I have are so good on English North America, and because we spend relatively little time on the colonial period in Loomis Chaffee's United States history course, I do not hesitate to combine American and world history in this manner.

To understand what happened when English people began to set up outposts and colonies in North America, we first have to understand the English backdrop. My hope is that in each of these group studies, students will search for the role played by ordinary people as well as that played by leaders. First we consider various primary readings from European literature and mythology prior to 1550 depicting their attitudes about the New World. Questions should arise about what these attitudes and visions would mean when different peoples came into increasing conflict with each other in the New World.

I then announce that the assessment for this unit is to be a letter in which students advise their close "friend," John Winthrop, whether or not to move to America, given the condition of England at the time.

Focal Issues

1. What was going on in England during the reigns of Elizabeth I, James I, and Charles I?
2. How were people and leaders responding to changes in their world?

Readings and Topics for Group Presentations

All read "From Subject to Citizen" background reading on James I and Charles I as leaders. Also assigned with the assessment is some background on John Winthrop's life as a Suffolk gentleman, and some excerpts from his journal.

1. The Religious Crisis: Puritans, Catholics, and Anglicans: documents and "From Subject to Citizen" articles on the religious policies and disputes between the Stuarts and religious dissenters, including the case of William Laud and the men who lost their ears
2. The Government's Financial Crisis: Monopolies, Subsidies, Loans, and Duties: "From Subject to Citizen" readings on the taxation question and how the House of Commons battled the Stuarts to keep the crown dependent on the landed gentry, while the crown tried to sidestep the law. Hampden's case is the focus (this group will debate Hampden's case for the class)
3. The Constitutional Crisis: Royal Prerogative and the Consent of Parliament—documents (including the Magna Carta) and background readings look back at England in the thirteenth century during the beginnings of Parliament, and relate those events to the attitudes of Elizabeth and the Stuarts (through speeches to Parliament by Elizabeth, James I, and Charles I)
4. Social Upheaval: The Birth of the Modern Class Structure—Peter Earle, "English Society," in *Stuart England*, Blair Worden, ed. (Oxford: Phaidon Press, 1986), 23–48 (analyzes the changing social structure in England toward a more urban class structure); and sections of Sumner Chilton Powell, *Puritan Village* (a study of the founding of Sudbury, Massachusetts—the selections focus on the life of Peter Noyes when he lived as a tenant farmer in Weyhill, England).

Investigation No. 2: Encounter and Change in the New World, 1607–1650

Continuing with English colonization as a case study, we look at encounters between diverse peoples and environments as the east coast of North America undergoes important changes in the early seventeenth century. Students will recognize the importance of factors such as the crises we have just studied, the spread of European diseases, the need for all peoples to adjust to economic as well as environmental factors, and the feelings of fear on all sides.

Focal Issues

1. How did visions, ambitions, traditions, environments, diseases, economics, and particular mixes of peoples combine to shape the various encounters that took place in America in the early seventeenth century?

2. What patterns set then would continue to be important in the lives of Americans in the years to come? Was this a story of the beginnings of democracy, or a story of European greed and racism?

Readings and Group Topics

1. The Algonkians enter the Atlantic Trading System: selections from John Smith, "The Indians of Virginia," documents by Roger Williams, Tecumseh, Red Jacket, Sir William Johnson, and a few Jesuit priests on Indian lifeways (with hints of recent changes as a result of the fur trade); chapter from William Cronon, *Changes in the Land* (discusses the impact of the fur trade and English and Algonkian agricultural practices on New England's ecosystem)

2. The Chesapeake Region: documents and articles about relations with the natives, the emergence of the tobacco economy, the head-right system, and the experiences of women

3. The Massachusetts Bay Colony: "From Subject to Citizen" readings on Winthrop's change in the charter to allow broader franchise, and on the banishment Roger Williams; selections from the trial transcript of Anne Hutchinson; excerpts from the Suffolk County court records and other documents on women in Massachusetts

4. The Connecticut Colony: "The Fundamental Orders of Connecticut," the 1650 Code of Laws, other background material that I have written on the various settlements that would become the Connecticut colony.

After the Connecticut group makes its presentation, I announce that we will look very closely at the Pequot War of 1637, which took place in Connecticut, but involved all of the New England colonies (see Figure 3–3). We study a number of primary sources (many of which offer conflicting accounts), and visit the Mashantucket Pequot Museum in Ledyard, Connecticut. From these resources I ask students to write a narrative history of the war that uses the other group presentations to give broader meaning and understanding of the event. (For a more detailed description of this exercise, see

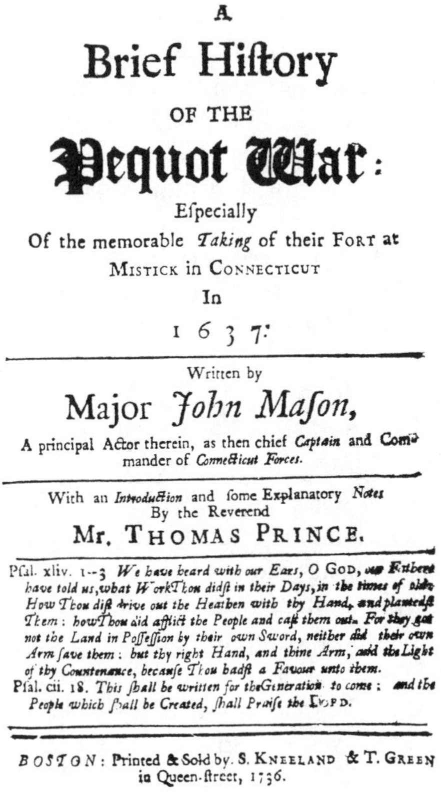

A

Brief Hiſtory

OF THE

𝔓equot 𝔚ar:

Eſpecially
Of the memorable *Taking* of their FORT at
MISTICK in CONNECTICUT

In

1 6 3 7:

Written by

Major *John Maſon,*

A principal Actor therein, as then chief *Captain* and Commander of *Connecticut Forces.*

With an *Introduction* and ſome Explanatory *Notes*
By the Reverend
Mr. THOMAS PRINCE.

Pſal. xliv. 1–3 *We have heard with our Ears, O GOD, our Fathers
have told us, what Work Thou didſt in their Days, in the times of old:
How Thou diſt drive out the Heathen with thy Hand, and plantedſt
Them : how Thou aid afflict the People and caſt them out. For they got
not the Land in Poſſeſſion by their own Sword, neither did their own
Arm ſave them : but thy right Hand, and thine Arm; and the Light
of thy Countenance, becauſe Thou hadſt a Favour unto them.*
Pſal. cii. 18. *This ſhall be written for the Generation to come : and the
People which ſhall be Created, ſhall Praiſe the LORD.*

BOSTON: Printed & Sold by. S. KNEELAND & T. GREEN
in Queen-ſtreet, 1736.

Figure 3–3. *Title page of John Mason's narrative of the Pequot War, 1637*

Chapter 6.) I take pains, at this point, to insist on careful interpretive work and critical thought, through which they distinguish biases in sources, consider point of view, balance secondary interpretation against primary source evidence, and give justification for their own interpretations. By this point in the course they should be far more competent as historical thinkers than they were when we first studied the English experience at Roanoak.

Interlude: Turmoil "at Home":
Civil War, Commonwealth, and Absolutism

In this section we return for a few days to Europe to see how events unfolded "at home," while a few Europeans were struggling to create outposts overseas. We begin with England and a simulation game (from "From Subject to Citizen" materials) that reviews Charles I's conflict with the House of Commons through the 1630s. This is followed by a role play of the Long Parliament, complete with a reenactment of Charles' bungled effort to arrest its ringleaders, and some reading on the English Civil War, capped by a film segment from *Cromwell* showing the King's trial and execution in 1649 (Alec Guinness is masterful as Charles Stuart, and Richard Harris does a good rendition of a somewhat fanatical Oliver Cromwell). We then read about the dilemmas Cromwell faced as Lord Protector, and about the "Restoration" of Charles II in 1660.

The years that followed were years in which the crown, not only in England but also in France under Louis XIV, gradually gained more and more control. Throughout the world this effort was expressed in the form of mercantilism, and in Europe, in the form of absolutism practiced by the later Stuarts, Louis XIV, Peter the Great, the Hapsburgs, and the Hohenzollerns. Only in England and the Netherlands were the landed gentry and merchant and professional classes strong enough, and was libertarian philosophy embraced enough, to mount a successful challenge to absolutism. Students should see, though, through examination of documents on absolutism, John Locke's philosophy, Parliament's installation of William and Mary, and the Laws of Trade and Navigation put in place by Cromwell, the Stuarts, and William and Mary's Parliament, that those rising to oppose absolute monarchy were no less mercantilist, no less authoritarian, and not much less aristocratic than the old nobility. Was this because those whom they ruled expected and allowed an autocratic ruling class? Or was this simply Marx's class conflict working its way through history? In the New World, colonies seemed to be involved in a trend toward a more democratic way of life—would this continue as the new aristocracy became more firmly entrenched in Europe? Locke had apparently been influenced by the evolution of political culture in America. Would his ideas last in a Europe becoming more and more marked by divisions between rich and poor, powerful and powerless? How would Louis XIV's notions of power play out in the French colonies of the New World? Where would the new Dutch aristocracy fit into the evolving world system? Students should certainly see how important these questions are. A notebook check here, particularly of their reflections, provides indications of learning about both the developments in Europe and study habits in general.

Investigation No. 3: Asia, Africa, and the Americas in the Seventeenth Century

Here we look at European expansion into other parts of the world besides English North America. Small groups use the library to research and develop reading selections themselves as a final term project. The topics are:

1. The East Indies and Japan (two very different responses to change in the world)
2. Central America and the Caribbean (a study in amalgamation and evolving social structure)
3. The St. Lawrence and Mississippi Valleys
4. West Africa

I am looking for students to come to an understanding of the seventeenth-century story in these places that relates what we have learned about Europe to the continuing encounters among different peoples and environments throughout the world. I will also be interested to see if they can recognize the importance of focusing on the perspective of the peoples who lived in these places prior to European arrival. Finally, I want students to consider the long-held assumption that European colonization in these places, emphasizing trade more than settlement, was fundamentally different from that on the eastern seaboard of North America. Was European colonization less intrusive, more respectful—or the opposite? Did indigenous structures and institutions last longer—or were the natives better equipped to repel European influence or attack?

Asking students to come forth with their own set of materials as a term-end project (especially primary sources with introductions written by the students) provides me not only with an indication of how much they are learning about the developments in these places in the seventeenth century, but also about differing perspectives on the emerging world system that was resulting from all the change of the past two centuries. As the students present their results, the degree to which other students take an interest in the presentations, ask questions, and make comments voluntarily also helps me to discern emerging attitudes about learning.

Part III: What's New in the New World?

Introduction: The Story of Olaudah Equiano

The introduction for this part of the course involves studying the story of Olaudah Equiano (also known as Gustavus Vassa). Olaudah was an African captured as a boy and sold into slavery in America. Later in life he achieved his freedom, and had his life story published by abolitionists who wanted to expose the evils of slavery. The excerpts that the students read provide enough of the story to raise a lot of questions about the way in which European expansion into the rest of the world developed in the century before the American Revolution.

In anticipation that my students will soon take an American history course, I feel an obligation to get them to see the emergence of societies in the Americas in the context of world history, that is, the coalescing of a world economic system, the struggle for worldwide commercial empires on the part of European nation-states, and the worldwide patterns of change and adaptation as peoples everywhere encountered new peoples, new ideas, and new environments.

Olaudah's story touches on all of these themes, especially in its connection of Africa and America, its relationship with the growing protest against slavery as the institution became more entrenched, and its portrayal of an individual caught in the flow of history. Finally, in presenting an individual who found himself in the lowest caste of the American social structure, but who eventually aspired toward a "good life" as defined by other Americans, the story raises the question, "What's new in the New World?" Hopefully the questions the story elicits will center around *institutions, structures, relationships,* and *values,* for these are the central foci for our understanding of the nature of the new societies emerging in the Americas. This is the theme of the term, as we try to understand what distinguished this particular New World from all the others that were shaping up around the earth.

Investigation No. 1: A New World in the Americas

One way to see how individuals, ideas, and environments mixed to create a New World in America is to study the emergence of various institutions and characteristics that historians have identified as distinctive of American society. Among these are participatory democracy, individualism, suspicion of authority, egalitarianism, and upward mobility.

As a whole class we first study the evolution of the New England town meeting, often viewed as the cradle of democracy. The basis of this study is Sumner Chilton Powell's research on Sudbury, Massachusetts, in which he finds that the town meeting originated from a combination of factors: traditional practices of seventeenth-century English villages, Puritan theology, the settlement of a population devoid of inherited status and shaken by diverse backgrounds, and the rigors of frontier life. All of these combined to shape new attitudes toward rank, class, and participation in decision making. Our focus is on the family heads of Sudbury who came from different regions of England and joined together to create their vision of community in Massachusetts Bay while civil war raged at "home." Issues of rank, land distribution, and farming practices could not be contained, however, producing not only division, but also more challenges to Old World practices and ideas than the founders of the community had counted on. We discover all this by acting out a town meeting on these issues that occurred in 1654. The bottom line is the complexity of the forces producing new ways in the New World.

From here we move to group work on four other examples of change resulting from a convergence of complex forces:

1. Virginia's "Meaner Sort" and Bacon's Rebellion of 1675: background reading (which I wrote) on the development of plantation society in Virginia; documents by Nathaniel Bacon and Governor Berkeley

2. Native Americans Resist—King Philip's War and the Pueblo Rebellion: documents narrating the story of both uprisings

3. Slavery Becomes an Institution: selections from the Virginia slave code of the late 1600s

4. The Outlanders: Salmon Brook (Connecticut), 1680–1713: two chapters from my own book, *A Tempest in a Small Town: The Myth and Reality of Country Life—Granby, Connecticut, 1680–1940* (Granby, CT: Salmon Brook Historical Society, 1996)

One thing to note as we work on these projects is that, whereas the Sudbury experience (and the reading on New England settlement in general) showed that New World society was becoming more democratic and egalitarian (as was the case in early Virginia), by the end of the seventeenth century those societies were actually becoming more stratified and there were more restrictions and fewer opportunities for those at the bottom of the social, economic, and political orders. Thus we note the complexity of New World evolution. As in the other parts of the course, the group presentations are followed by individual papers focusing, this time, on the evolution of democracy in the New World.

Investigation No. 2: The Great Forced Migration and Changes for Africa

Here we study materials designed to help students understand the evolution of the slave trade as it reached its peak in the early 1700s. How many people were involved? What effect did the removal of all these people have on Africa? Why would Africans participate in the slave trade themselves? What was in it for them? Were they any different from the Europeans? In daily group work we do some analysis of documents and maps in order to understand how much the slave trade had come to dominate African commerce, and politics for that matter, in the early eighteenth century. This is followed by a role play in which various students in the class play different individuals with different perspectives on the situation in West Africa in the early 1700s (for a detailed description of this role play, see Chapter 6).

Interlude: The Struggle for World Empire

This next brief section involves a look at the association between mercantilism and conflict among nation-states, as competition for commercial and strategic advantage throughout the world grew more intense in the late seventeenth and early eighteenth centuries. The reading presents some background on the wars between 1690 and the Peace of Utrecht in 1713. This will help students ask questions about what was going on in the world outside of North America and whether other peoples were experiencing the same patterns of change. Was the whole world a frontier as the nation-states fought for control of it? A notebook check here will show if students have become good at the study habits taught in the course, and are able to put together information on varying topics in their reflections to construct a sensible narrative on their own.

We follow this with the "Game of Empire," a simulation of the Atlantic trading system originally developed as part of "From Subject to Citizen." In this game students become trading "interest groups": London Merchants, European Merchants, West African Traders, Algonkian Trappers, West Indies Planters, Southern Planters, Colonial Farmers, or New England Merchants. As such they trade and ship their products around the Atlantic, trying to acquire a prescribed number of imports that they need. They must deal with risks such as pirates, storms, and confiscations of cargoes that violate the British Laws of Trade and Navigation. (I have elaborated on the original version of this game, adding some interest groups, and developing a Filemaker Pro file that handles the transactions and posts accounts and warehouse holdings on classroom computer screens, to provide a stock-exchange ambience. It really is a madhouse.) After playing the game students should understand how mercantilism thoroughly transformed the Atlantic rim and brought about a unique mixing of peoples in the Americas as well as a great exchange of products. With this in mind we take a trip to Boston and Salem to help visualize the impact of the world of sea commerce on the emergence of the American society.

Investigation No. 3: New Ideas in a New World

The mixing of peoples, traditions, visions, and environments created a new society in North America. In this group investigation students get a sense of many of the new elements that are becoming part of being an American. The four group topics are:

1. The Social Structure of the Atlantic Colonies—including some understanding of how the Enlightenment shaped ideas among the upper
   classes with a look at William Byrd, Cotton Mather, and Benjamin
   Franklin (excerpts from their respective journals); and a look at groups
   such as Jews, the Scotch-Irish, the Germans, and other non-British
   groups who brought their cultural baggage to the British colonies (a
   collection of statistics and travelers' descriptions)

2. The Great Awakening—a religious upheaval in the early eighteenth
   century with widespread impact; readings from sermons and letters of
   participants

3. The Continuing Saga of Salmon Brook in Connecticut—two more
   chapters from *A Tempest in a Small Town,* which describe the settlement's growth and development through land distribution controver-
   sies, threats of attack from the north, and the turmoil of the Great
   Awakening

4. Echoes of African religion in a Christian world—reading from Albert
   Raboteau, *Slave Religion: The "Invisible Institution" in The Antebellum
   South.*

As an assessment for this investigation I ask students to become Michel
Crèvecoeur, whom I have converted into a French spy, ordered by Governor
Duquesne of Canada to infiltrate the British seaboard colonies in North
America and to write a report on "what makes Americans tick" (so the governor can decide if it would be a good idea to attack at this point). They are to
analyze the strengths and weaknesses of the society, and should be struck by
the remarkable diversity, cultural dislocation, and economic strength, even as
its leaders are trying to establish unchallenged hegemony. (This assignment is
given in full in Chapter 6.)

Conclusion: Rebellion

We conclude the course with a look at two rebellions, Peter Zenger's publication of antigovernment news stories in New York in 1733 and the Stono River
Rebellion in Georgia in 1739. Both of these help to solidify our understanding of the tumultuous impact of European expansion and all of the conflict,
change, and new thinking that it engendered. The rebellions thus offer much
food for thought on the central issue of "What's new in the New World?"
Since this question encapsulates many of the processes of adaptation and
change we have studied during the year, I ask students for a final essay addressing the topic. In addition, I ask them to revisit one of their former papers

or reflections that they feel represents an important learning experience for them and to sharpen and refine this piece of writing.

In "The World After Columbus" students learn a lot about a little. That is, while no one-year course of study can adequately cover all nine eras defined in the world history section of the *National Standards for History*, this course does not even claim to cover its fair share! What "The World After Columbus" does claim to accomplish, however, is to make its students lifetime learners. First, by engaging them in the study of exciting and cataclysmic events through a variety of student-centered imaginative activities, the experience shows kids that history is fun, intriguing, and based on the sometimes tragic and sometimes triumphant lives of real people. Second, by reaching backward into former eras and forward into the present in establishing relationships and connections, the course awakens students to the immensity of human history that is deserving of careful and imaginative study and inquiry. The idea is to encourage students to select history courses in the future that address these other eras and themes, or to stimulate in them enough interest to want to learn more about history on their own. Finally, by providing them with skills in critical thought and inquiry through months of exercises revolving around the fundamentals of historical thinking, the course gives them the ability and confidence to undertake the lifelong study of history and to appreciate and understand human experience at its most complex levels. The three centuries after 1492 was an era of new worlds, and in this course kids discover a new world of exploration into the past.

Notes

1. National Center for History in the Schools, *National Standards for History*, Basic Edition (Los Angeles: National Center for History in the Schools, 1996); *Curriculum Standards for Social Studies: Expectations of Excellence*, National Council for the Social Studies (1994), available: http://www.ncss.org /standards/home.html. See also *Building a History Curriculum: Guidelines for Teaching History in Schools* (Bradley Commission on History in Schools, 1988).

2. See *National Standards for History*, Chapter 2.

3. See *National Standards for History*, 76–84, 174–84.

4. Quite a few strategies in this course (including the use of the "Lost Colony" case in the introduction) are borrowed from an older course I taught for many years called "From Subject to Citizen." This course was created by the Educational Development Committee in Cambridge, Massachusetts, in the late 1960s (Nona Plesser Lyons was the director). The EDC courses were part of the

"New Social Studies" movement, and inspired largely by the ideas of Jerome Bruner. "The World After Columbus" evolved as I taught "From Subject to Citizen" over the years, emerging finally with its global context and cultural orientation, as opposed to the Anglo-American constitutional focus of the original course. Nevertheless, I have incorporated much of the pedagogy behind "From Subject to Citizen" into this course.

4

Beyond Eurocentrism
The View from the "Non-West"

LOU RATTÉ

There are more things in heaven and earth, Horatio, than are dreamt of in your philosophy.

The more we learn about the past, the more surprised we ought to be about our own ignorance. As we begin to feel comfortable with a new subject we're likely to ask: "How could I possibly not have known that?" Then comes the more interesting set of questions: "Since I didn't know that, why do I know what I do know? How did I come to know this rather than that?" Since the early 1980s I have had students read excerpts from Edward Said's *Orientalism.* My own favorite section of the book is in the introduction under the subheading of "The Personal Dimension." There Said quotes Antonio Gramsci: "The starting-point of critical elaboration is the consciousness of what one really is, and is 'knowing thyself' as a product of the historical process to date, which has deposited in you an infinity of traces, without leaving an inventory."[1] Said urges us to think of ourselves as historical players and take that inventory of the traces that history has left on us, traces that presumably can tell us something about why we know what we know, and why we don't know many things that we might know.

Edward Said, I have to say, is not students' favorite reading. Now, more than twenty years after the publication of the book, his message appears both too obvious and far too obscure for students. On the one hand, students have no trouble assenting to the idea that scholars, writers, painters, colonial administrators, even poets could represent the interests of ruling elites in their works; on the other hand, students in upper-level high school courses and

94

lower-level college courses have difficulty thinking about any restrictions on their own thinking, or, as one student put it, seeing themselves as having been "formatted" by society. Students read bits of Edward Said's text and wonder what all the fuss is about. *Orientalism* does not strike today's students with the hammer blow that the book delivered to many scholars when it was first published.

What was all the fuss about? Since the publication of *Orientalism* in 1978, the study of colonialism has become one of the hottest subjects in American academia. All of this interest is not, of course, due to Edward Said, but his book can serve as a good place to start. During the last two decades, in established disciplines, in interdisciplinary work, and in work carried out under new disciplinary labels (colonial history, cultural studies, postcolonial studies), scholars have questioned the status of the knowledge that we in the West have about the rest of the world. Most of what we know, most of what has been available for us to know, is the work of people who have had some tie to colonialism. The implications of the argument are vast, and they surely are relevant to the work of teaching world history; but how are they relevant? This issue is what I want to explore in this chapter.

Historians work within frames that give coherence to their arguments and interpretations, and much of the critical work in history, anthropology, and literary studies over the past two decades has helped us to understand the pervasiveness and strength of the Eurocentric frame for understanding history within which we all have worked. James Blaut, perhaps, puts it most simply: in the Eurocentric worldview, some inner dynamic in European society is said to be responsible for Europe's astonishing rise to world power and dominance after 1492, and the history of the rest of the world after that is the history of all areas being brought in, one by one, under the benevolent tutelage of the West.[2] There are many different ways of telling this same story of immense cultural power, and all point to a core perception. Eurocentrism inhabits our thinking, is our common sense of how the world is: attack one aspect of it and, like the balloon man who pops up again when you knock him over, it remains as strong as ever.

During the last two decades, scholars who specialize in areas around the world have mounted critiques of knowledge constructed during the period of European world dominance. Their work has been complemented by critiques of American scholarship on world areas after World War II and through the era of the Cold War. In the wake of these critiques, a new generation of scholars has taken up the task of dismantling, piece by piece, those constructions of the past that have been called into question. These critical and deconstructive efforts are now bearing fruit in the work of scholars who are mapping out new kinds of questions and issues to explore, sometimes with entirely new casts of characters. Teachers of world history cannot master this body of new scholarship all at once, in ways that will enable them to use it to shape what and how they teach. Where should they start? What are the most significant issues to raise at the beginning of the exploration? In what follows I suggest some of the strategies I have used to help students and teachers learn where scholars have made their most startling discoveries.

The Primary Source

If Eurocentrism implies seeing the world from the perspective of Europe, it would seem that if we introduce primary sources from other parts of the world into the world survey we will solve at least part of the problem. Once we entertain the possibilities implicit in the critique of Western knowledge about the rest of the world, we have a serious problem with the primary source, though.

Many teachers have thought to give voice to peoples from around the world by introducing primary sources, and the problem is not with the source but *with how it will be read.* If we are inside a Eurocentric frame, how will we read a text from outside that frame other than to bring it into our frame? The principal means for doing so, of course, is through translation. I remember well when I was learning to read Bengali and working with a young graduate student. I was translating some passages from a novel by Rabindranath Tagore and I knew enough to make out the words but needed help in putting together the sentences. In a particular passage Tagore mentioned a variety of gods and goddesses, all named. My tutor translated the whole list of deities as "God." When I questioned her, she responded, "Well, if it were written in English, this is what it would say." This was an alarming introduction to biculturalism and the politics of translation. We are not used to thinking that as English speakers we are at a disadvantage when it comes to learning about the rest of the world. What would happen to our sense of security about what we know if we stopped to think about how all those British colonials, on whose empire the sun never set, acquired their knowledge? Supposing all the "native informants" who provided the Europeans with basic information about the colonized society were behaving as my tutor had done? Native informants, after all, got their positions because they knew the language of the colonizer.

As I began to think about the idea that we who have grown up in the West know less about the world than we think we do, and that our ignorance is not completely accidental, I tried to devise ways to help teachers and students reach the same point. One of the devices, which I used with sixth graders and their teachers, as well as with other students, was to select pages from various English–foreign language dictionaries and ask students to find the translation of particular words. Students have no problem with the English-French, English-Spanish, and English-German pages, but when they get to the English-Sanskrit, English-Bengali, and English-Arabic pages, and have to deal with different alphabets, they ask what's going on. "We can't read this!" That, of course, is the point. Students ought to begin their study of world history with an awareness that their linguistic insufficiencies will get in the way of their knowing everything they might like to know.

Many of our teaching practices, undertaken with the best of motives, turn out not to be as neutral as we think. In the early stages of enthusiasm for multiculturalism, simplified versions of *Ramayana* in English translation became popular, especially for young students. What was the point of having young students read *Ramayana,* especially in those curricular circumstances where it was either the only Indian offering, or was encased in generalizations that spanned the course of Indian history? Surely the point was to acquire "cultural literacy," that is, to be able to identify the story as an Indian story, much as textbook illustrations encourage their users to recognize sculptures of many-armed figures as Indian. We can call this the Quiz Kid approach to world studies. This is the way, at the elementary level, we have come to "read" India, but is this the best we can do? Here a logical rejoinder might be: but isn't this what we do with Greek mythology?

It is, of course, true, that Hector and Achilles are not necessarily more familiar to American schoolchildren than Rama and Sita, but we can assume that by the time those students reach high school, and certainly by the time they reach college, ancient Greece will have become familiar in a variety of ways, even if a major vehicle of transmission is the Disney movie. Students will know something, however rudimentary (and even incorrect from an academic perspective), about Greek architecture, Greek drama, Greek mythology, Athenian polity, and the Athenian golden age. The effect will be that when students are given texts to read, they will be able to read them within what, for them, is a known cultural context. These icons of our Greek inheritance have been "naturalized" for them. Students will be able to read and feel, at least, that they know what the text says and why it says it in that particular way. They will know that the people represented in the text are full human beings, like themselves.

American students cannot impose that same sense of familiarity, of cultural ownership, over texts from India, Japan, Southeast Asia, West Africa, Latin America, and every other place that is not part of what we claim as Western culture. Lacking that perhaps mistaken sense of cultural familiarity, students, teachers, all of us, will tend to read texts from elsewhere as examples of how they do things over there, as manifestations of Otherness.

Starting with the Present: India

If we want to distance ourselves from the temptation to treat people as the products of their culture in too simplistic a way, I suggest beginning with materials that make it difficult to distinguish the place of origin. In teaching about India, I have tried this approach by using works by twentieth-century Indian artists.

There are a great many painters in India today, and indeed a great deal of art criticism in English and other Indian languages. There is a network of galleries and museums linking India's major cities and art centers, and a full calendar of yearly exhibitions. A few years ago, Americans in general knew little or nothing about this modern institutionalization of art production and consumption in India. Few of us were exempt from this general ignorance. I remember telling an Indologist friend of mine that I was doing some research on modern art in India and she responded, "I didn't know they had any modern art."

To gather materials I have used Indian art journals and magazines, art histories, artists' biographies, and museum and exhibition catalogues. My goal has been to give students a taste of what Indians have been painting for a hundred years. I have shown slides and also made color copies, which I have then had laminated so that they can be handed around in the classroom. Both slides and laminated photographs work well, and the color laminations have the added advantage that students can handle them and put them together in ways that I hadn't thought of. I have generally presented the images chronologically, while more visually sensitive students will see many other possibilities. Laminated images can be tacked up for the whole of the time we are talking about India, serving as a constant reminder that there are Indian perspectives on anything about the subcontinent that we are likely to touch upon. As a culminating exercise, students can use the laminated images to mount their own exhibition.

The point of using visual images rather than texts is that they can be looked at quickly and the whole taken in, in ways that, for my purposes, are more efficient than having students pore over written materials. The process of viewing is social and students are encouraged to talk about what they see. I want students to be able to move on from this initial exposure to India with that same sense of familiarity that they bring to their study of ancient Greece. Later they can develop a more complex picture of the history and culture of the subcontinent.

It is generally understood in the field of Indian art history that the great stone and bronze sculptural traditions that we have come to identify as classical Indian art had come to an end before the establishment of British rule. Architecture and painting flourished under Moghul rule and the miniature tradition in painting thrived in several independent princedoms throughout the subcontinent as well as in Moghul courts well into the nineteenth century. As British rule extended its range, however, these older sources of patronage dried up and the miniature tradition suffered. The British government became an art patron of a sort, at the very time when there was a good deal of debate in British Indian circles about whether India had a fine arts tradition at all, or whether what Indian artists had contributed to the world ought to be classified as ornament. Following out the logic of this debate, the imperial government established art schools for Indians in the three major colonial cities of Bombay, Calcutta, and Madras, in which aspiring Indian artists could be trained in surveying techniques and the design of industrial products. With the rise of nationalist consciousness in the late nineteenth century this dreary scenario began to change. Led by Indian artists and British sympathizers, the art schools became sites for cultural revival. Painters turned first to the miniaturist schools, and attempted to paint in that style; then there was an attempt to paint in the folk tradition. By the 1920s artists who were familiar with trends in Europe broke away from the early revivalist constraints to produce abstract art. By the 1930s Indian artists were finding their way to Paris and came home to produce works that, stylistically, could not be distinguished from those of their European and American contemporaries. Twentieth-century Indian art includes works that treat modern subject matter in ways that do not signal the artist's national or cultural identity; works that consciously attempt, stylistically, to be "Indian"; and works that use every available technique to represent aspects of contemporary Indian life.

When I first began to use examples of this body of work, I called the presentation "the shock of the familiar." This was a conscious reversal of what I had been taught was the appropriate approach to teaching about another culture, which was to generate "the shock of the unfamiliar." We were then teaching cultural difference, and we wanted to simulate the experience of culture shock in the classroom. Seeing twentieth-century Indian works in chronological order, from the beginnings of the revival up to the present, does give the viewer a peculiar feeling of familiarity. The attempts at reviving the miniaturist tradition may not strike any chords for today's students, but the attempts of professional artists to work in folk traditions generally do. Here can be found the familiar bullock cart heading off into the sunset; the women coming home from the well with water jugs on their heads, saris blowing in the breeze; children scantily clad playing in the center of a village scene. Then comes the punch. What are these cubist pictures doing here? What are these abstractions? What is surrealism doing in this collection? The paintings do not look "Indian." They look modern. Even students who claim to be ignorant of modern art will ask, "Why are they painting like that? That looks Western; why aren't they painting like Indians?" Creating a sense of the familiar has the desired effect of bringing embedded cultural assumptions to the surface. At this point I might return to Edward Said and his idea about taking an inventory of the "traces" history has left on us. "How do you know how Indians should paint?" I might ask. "What do you mean when you say the pictures look 'Western'?"

Enabling students to have a response that reveals that they have some expectations about how Indians are supposed to be can move us very quickly into a place where we are ready to explore the work of contemporary scholars. I am thinking about that large and fast-growing body of contemporary scholarship that explores how European colonizers and Europeans in general participated in the long process of representing colonial subjects as "Others," and how scholars are now challenging that view. The "Otherness" of Indians, as the group in question here, has become part of our own cultural orientation, and American high school and college students will certainly have imbibed it. As "Others," Indians are religious, otherworldly, fatalistic, poor, caste-ridden, village oriented, and apolitical. It is this cultural baggage that gets summoned to the surface when students react with surprise to the works of contemporary Indian painters. Implicit in the response is the assumption that the painters should be painting in a way appropriate to Indians; they should be making something that *we* can recognize as Indian. Under no circumstances should they be modern.

As a thought experiment, let us challenge the assumption that many new teachers of world history hold when they say that they know nothing about the new subject, be it India, Japan, or West Africa, when the time approaches to introduce it into the survey. Supposing we ask them to return in memory to their childhood. Recent scholarship on children's literature and popular culture provides insights into what such characters as Tarzan, Tin Tin, Babar, and Donald Duck and his nephews deliver to young readers.[3] These heroes of our collective youth took us around the world to places where they knew more and always outsmarted the natives. Just as we pick up some sense of our culture's long interest in Greek culture simply by growing up in the United States, we all pick up a good deal more than we think we do about the rest of the world. As teachers, we may think we can easily put all those childish things aside, but it is not as easy as we think. The books in which these beloved characters of childhood appear, and many others like them, set the stage for lumping together all parts of the world that are not western Europe and the United States. At the academic level, these books help to legitimize courses in the "non-West." It is probably not an exaggeration to say that many Americans grow up already knowing that the world is divided into "us" and "them," in possession of what James Blaut calls a sense of the inside and the outside and what scholars of colonialism call Europe (and the United States) and its

Others. When Edward Said talks about the sheer knitted togetherness of the colonial discourse, he has something of this fabric woven in childhood in mind.

If I am right in assuming that teachers, as adults in American society, have come to see the world in ways that are presupposed by these colonial structures, then our agenda as world history teachers becomes a little clearer. We need to approach the subjects we teach about with a dual purpose in mind: (1) we need to ask what we can know and teach about the subject; and (2) we need to examine what predispositions we have imbibed that may block our own understanding. In the case of India, for instance, we might ask of world history texts why India is relegated to a slot in the ancient civilization section. European Orientalist scholarship on India, from the late eighteenth century on, produced an historical representation of the whole of the sub-continent that supplied it with a golden age in the distant past, followed by a period of cultural decline, culminating in political and cultural anarchy in the eighteenth century. At that low point in its history, according to the standard Orientalist view, India fell under British rule; the British brought law, order, and the Pax Britannica, and set the people on the road toward modernization. Presenting the golden age before decline, after which follows foreign colo-nization, has been part of the "Civilizations" approach in world history. Is this the way Indians see their own history?

Scenarios such as this one on India's golden age are hard to break into, primarily because we hold them unconsciously. One way to avoid setting them in motion, in the case of India, is to start with the Indian present, or, as I have suggested, the twentieth century. Many of the painters do fulfill our ex-pectations of what pictures of India should look like: village scenes peopled with men, women, and children in obviously non-Western clothing; but some of the same painters who turned out pictures of that sort also produced cubist representations of the modern city, and works exploring the modern psyche. One Indian painter whose work I studied started his career in the late nine-teenth century painting European-style landscapes. Then for a short while he joined with other Indian painters in the effort to revive the miniature tradition. He finally developed what became his distinctive style when he combined the approach of European moderns like Matisse with that of un-schooled urban painters in his home city of Calcutta.[4] There is enough here to introduce questions about hybridity, identity, and subjecthood for which the scholarly archive is large. The issues raised can also be more extensively addressed by advanced students by reading Indian art criticism.[5]

What can be valuable in the exercise of using twentieth-century Indian images is that it can help teachers as well as their students begin to construct a new frame for inquiring about the world, even as they recognize the need to question the old frame they have inherited. For instance, we used to think about modernity and culture as two unconnected subjects. The West was modern and the rest of the world had culture. When what the rest of the world does fails to meet our expectations, we get confused. Critics of twentieth-century Indian art have asked: why were they painting like that? What were they trying to prove? Why didn't they stick to their own traditions? Why did they copy Europeans? Why don't these paintings tell us about Indian life? Well, of course, they do; it just isn't the Indian life we thought we wanted to know about.

Approaching the Past: India

Seeing the present of places we teach about in the world survey as more culturally complicated than we thought can also help us in approaching the past of these places in more nuanced fashion. The first step is to become more critically aware of how the past is presented to us. Again, my example is from India.

As I said in Chapter 2, Banaras was one of the cities included in the sixth-grade curriculum. While we were working on the second draft of the curriculum, the nearby Yale University art gallery was hosting a traveling exhibition from the Asia Society, titled *The Cosmic Dancer: Shiva Nataraja*. Everyone concerned with the curriculum project wanted to take students to the exhibition, and now I want to address the question of why. What ought to be our goals in attempting to integrate museum and exhibition going into student learning?

In treating art as illustrative of some other theme or narrative point, we historians have perpetuated practices that in recent years have come under scholarly scrutiny. We assume it is a good thing to bring art into the world history curriculum at all levels, but why? On what grounds do we make that assumption? One of the most commonplace of classroom practices is to present art from outside Europe as representative of the culture. Like using *Ramayana* as the emblematic Indian text, the practice of showing a few slides of classical Indian art in a world survey tends to trigger those responses that call up the whole scenario of greatness followed by decline, with the British imperialists waiting to revive the dying giant. We assume the pieces to be transparent embodiments of cultural truth. Europe and America may have history, and dynamic movement through time, but India has stasis, tradition, culture. What this construction of India has meant is that any artifact, written text, or material object can be read as though it gave access to the whole. We think we are learning important things about the culture by being able to recognize its icons. We fail to recognize that we, in the collective sense, have created the icon. I remember two Indian friends of mine talking about their days as graduate students at Cornell. They were both asked by the graduate student league to talk about Hinduism. The wife wrote home to her father who rushed back a telegram saying, "Refuse! You know nothing about Hinduism." The husband, on the other hand, reports that he went to the Cornell library, looked up some books by American scholars on Hinduism, and gave the assembled group what they were able to hear.

The Yale University's presentation of Chola-period Natarajas from the Rockefeller collection, owned by the Asia Society, was staggeringly beautiful. The objects, several well over two feet high, were placed on blocks with the top at or below eye level, and the larger pieces were exposed, unprotected. Intimacy, just short of reaching out and touching, was a key goal of the exhibition. The brochure accompanying the exhibition introduced Shiva as Lord of the Dance, identified the figure of Shiva Nataraj with the Chola period (880–1279), provided information on the Chola kings as temple builders and art patrons, and described the *cire perdue* (lost wax) process used by the Chola bronze sculptors.[6] The author then explicated the meaning of Dancing Shiva, told about other forms of Shiva, introduced Shiva's family and several prominent South Indian Saivite devotees, and made some general statements about Hinduism, which began "Hindus worship . . . ," "Much Hindu worship occurs . . . ," "Hinduism pervades . . . ," and "In Hinduism . . ."

What I found troubling about this brochure of some sixteen pages, in the context of a stunning and stunningly accessible exhibition, was that it was not at all unusual. This type of presentation has been standard museum practice: enter the gallery ignorant and come out knowing about the culture. The brochure provides a way of reading the images that moves us effortlessly from Shiva, to a mythological context, to Hinduism as the key to grasping India in its totality. The objects themselves are effectively muted. How can we block that process before it starts?

The centerpieces of the show were several Chola-period Natarajas. Along with these masterpieces were Chola-period works representing Shiva in manifestations other than as Lord of the Dance, images of Parvati, Shiva's wife, and their children, and images of devotees. Finally, there was a series of small objects identified as pieces used in private worship, and objects from India, Tibet, Nepal, and East Java showing the importance of the dance in Indian culture. The earliest pieces were from the seventh century, and the latest from the sixteenth century.

The chronological and geographical span represented by the objects served to blur the centrality of the Chola pieces and their specific history, reinforcing a sense of timelessness. It was important to overcome that perception, which in this case we could do by providing students with materials that would encourage them to focus on people and the production of images.

Documentation on the Chola Nataraj tells us that the figure of the dancing Shiva encircled by a ring of fire was most probably invented in a royal workshop presided over by Queen Sembiyan Mahadevi.[7] Queen Sembiyan Mahadevi was married to King Gandaraditya, who ruled the Chola Empire from 949 to 957. Queen Sembiyan lived for nearly half a century after her husband's death, herself dying in 1006. Between the death of her husband in 957 and the assumption of rule by her son, Uttama Chola, in 969, Sembiyan Mahadevi was apparently respected but not particularly active as a patron of the arts. When Uttama Chola became emperor his mother presided over the royal workshop, and in that workshop under Sembiyan Mahadevi's patronage the figure of Shiva Nataraj was invented.

Today, Shiva Nataraj is most probably familiar to our students as the identifying icon on Indian restaurant menus. Whoever thinks to ask where the image came from and how it came to be in the first place? How did this particular form move from three-dimensional sculpture to two-dimensional print, and how did it come to be so well known in America?[8]

Our sixth-grade students went to the Yale show having already seen pictures of the objects they would be viewing and with a host of questions aimed at helping them analyze the aim of the exhibition. This, of course, is not a process of preparation limited to elementary school children. Students of all ages can learn that there is intention behind the display of objects. Before students go to an exhibition they should be armed with questions that will help them decipher the intention: what does the designer or curator want to show? When and where were the objects made? How are the objects categorized? What might be the purpose of the exhibit? Learning to see exhibitions themselves as "texts" that can be read can be another point of entry for teachers and students into the world of contemporary scholarship. Why have scholars begun to question museum practice? What is involved in showing objects from various places around the world? How are such objects differentiated one from another, and categorized? What distinguishes art from craft? How did the objects that we see in our museums come to be there? This last question can open up a whole range of inquiry about the history of objects, the story of their "social life," the tale of how they are moved from one part of the world to another, and what happens in the transit.[9]

A major benefit, with broad applicability, of approaching museum exhibitions with a critical posture is that they can provide at least partially visible evidence of how knowledge is constructed. On the one hand is the object; on the other the brochure, label, catalogue, critical review. How are these two sets related to each other? As I have pondered this question in a variety of different textual circumstances, I find my admiration growing for those late eighteenth- and nineteenth-century British colonials who went out to India (as they used to say) and categorized everything they saw, touched, unearthed, or heard about. How did they manage to pull it off? What gave them such tremendous confidence in their abilities? How did they get from the ignorant confusion of first encounters to the authoritative pronouncements that we have inherited today, which enable us to begin sentences with "Hinduism is . . ."? When students and teachers begin to ask these questions they are ready to turn to Edward Said and begin to think about what the term "Orientalism" implies.

One of the ways I have tried to get students to think about the work of the early Orientalists is to ask them what they think is the best way to learn about a new place. They walk right into the trap: "Go there, of course. Learn firsthand from the people." I then show some slides of a contemporary Indian city and ask students to imagine what they think they would do when they got off the plane. What if the people they approached did not speak English? What would it mean if the people *did* speak English? What if nobody stopped to talk? How would they make sense out of what they were seeing? Of course, for imperial rulers it was easier than it would be for today's young traveler. The means for constructing knowledge were, so to speak, all shipped around in the equivalent of the diplomatic pouch.

Instead of presenting art objects as illustrative of culture, following imperial patterns for exhibiting that have evolved in the nineteenth century, we might start with helping students ask questions about how objects came to be produced, and what we can know about their site of production. Who were they produced for, and what do we know about how their original viewers perceived them? What are the circumstances under which we are viewing them? This last question is particularly important. Often the accompanying literature will try to make us feel that the object itself can carry us, in imagination, to the original place of production, can endow us with the capacity to see as did the first viewer. In fact, we are seeing the work not as ritual or sacred object, but as art. We should always make that point clear to students.

The "Contact Zone": West Africa

Classifying objects from outside the Euro-American culture area as art, rather than craft or ornament, is actually quite a recent phenomenon in colonial history. There is a good deal of scholarship on the collection, presentation, and interpretation of objects from around the world in ethnographic museums, cabinets of curiosities, and world's fairs. Within that scholarship there is a growing consensus that the categorizing schemes employed in these places of exhibition were initially derived from ways of classifying data from the natural world that emerged from the European Enlightenment. While the categorizers assumed that objects collected from particular locations could convey some sort of inherent meaning, today's scholars assume that the organization scheme imposed by the classificatory taxonomy *helped to produce the meaning it was designed to describe.* Insofar as we are inclined to identify with those collectors and classifiers, we can say that the nineteenth-century interpretive schema for classifying and categorizing objects from around the world tell us a good deal about ourselves; but what do they tell us about the rest of the world? They tell us more than we might initially think, but we have to be ready to ask the right questions. Recent scholarship ought to be our guide.

Two major nineteenth-century tropes for thinking about the pasts of places outside Europe and America were the model of decline from greatness to decadence, which applied to India, and the model of primitive stasis, which applied to Africa. What critical scholarship calls our attention to is the critical framing. By challenging notions of decadence and of primitive stasis as adequate explanatory devices, we are well on the way to being able to benefit from recent scholarship.

In the case of India I have suggested the usefulness of studying twentieth-century painting to help teachers as well as students move beyond their own expectations of the exotic and the strange. In the case of West Africa, recent studies of how objects move from the place of production to the place of consumption can be particularly provocative.

Since the early twentieth century when artists in Paris discovered West African masks and attempted to perceive the secret behind the representation, objects from West Africa have been in demand among collectors in the West. Why? What do these objects mean to the Western collector? If the Chola Nataraj can deliver India to the viewer, what does the mask from West Africa deliver? To make the point dramatically, that meaning is constructed rather than inherent or discovered, anthropologist Christopher Steiner writes: "Because the symbols of African art are silent outside their original community of spokespersons, the objects are themselves tabula rasa—virgin icons, upon which observers imprint their own significance and interpretation."[10]

Can it be so simple? Can the observer just make it up? Obviously not; as Steiner describes it, the process of imprinting on the object is a long and complicated one in which knowledge is mediated by third parties who bring together the meanings surrounding the making of objects with the expectations of buyers far removed from the place of production. The process Steiner describes reminds me of my experience with the Bengali translator: the mediator has experience of both sides. A process of translation goes on, even though it may not necessarily be from one language to another.

People who study India have long joked about Max Müller, the great nineteenth-century Sanskritist, who never went to India. When asked why, Müller is supposed to have said, "I prefer the Banaras of the mind." If true, Müller preferred the pure form derived from the study of texts, over the messy reality of the nineteenth-century city he would have encountered had he made the trip. Whatever Müller thought about the real city of Banaras, many nineteenth- and early twentieth-century anthropologists, travel writers, tourists, and colonial officials thought they were witnessing the death agony of traditional cultures being daily brought into contact with the dynamic West. Many thought that through writing and drawing, later photographing, they were preserving the lifeways of groups soon to become extinct. As the idea of cultural extinction took hold, objects assigned to the precontact period increased in value.

From these views, we inherit our collective nostalgia for a world before European contact. Sub-Saharan Africa, and West Africa in particular, has fascinated Euro-American imagination, and objects from it have been endowed with particular evocative power. These objects apparently fulfill some deep need or desire that obviates the need for firsthand experience, just as Müller's Sanskrit texts did for him. To make this point Steiner writes about and quotes a collector of African art:

> This first experience with African art reveals a touch of the romantic nature that [this collector of African art] feels goes hand in hand with his collecting. Further evidence of this can be heard in the reason he gives for feeling that going to Africa is not necessary to his collecting. He views his objects, he says, as being conceived in the pre-colonial aesthetic that he admires. He adds that "if Addidas (sic) sneakers and Sony walkmen were absent from the Ivory Coast, I might reconsider my position, but, at present, my romantic vision of precolonial Ivory Coast is too fragile to tamper with."[11]

Imagine yourself as a West African art trader. What would be your reaction to this collector's fantasy? The Western market for West African objects, Steiner tells us, developed in the second decade of the twentieth century. Apparently, by the 1920s, or about a decade after the takeoff, artists and traders in West Africa began to organize the supply side of the exchange. Artists began to make objects for the export market and traders began to develop techniques for selling. These included artificially aging objects and adopting a variety of means to play to the buyer's expectations. If the buyer wanted an object that had been used in village rituals, oil could be rubbed on the inside of the mask to make it appear that a dancer had sweated into it. If the buyer thought the trader to be just an ignorant middle man unaware of the value of his wares, the trader could hide some objects in a corner and let the buyer discover them on his own.

In this study of the African art market we have a suggestion of why we should concentrate on the present of world areas as we introduce them into the survey. Anthropologists are no longer looking for a timeless present before contact, and historians have turned a critical eye on the explanatory narratives of the past. Most important, scholarship has given us much greater potential access to people who we might not have considered as worthy of inclusion in a survey. These very people, seemingly ordinary and outside the great seats of action, are turning out to be the ones who can shed light on the important processes that have shaped our understanding. In many studies that look at meaning making among nondominant groups, we get a sense of how ordinary people have acted in history in ways that have actually colluded in enabling us in the West to continue to think fantastic thoughts about them because it was in their interest to have it so.

Students find the West African art traders, as Steiner presents them, to be fascinating because they are so familiar, so very like ourselves. Any inclination toward ascribing romantic exoticism, primitivism, or backwardness to the Africa that the traders represent is effectively blocked. Role playing in order to understand the process of how objects are commodified as they move from African workshop to museum vitrine or household shelf in the West works particularly well here.

Extending the Comparative Range: Meiji Japan

Once we get a feel for the Western-originated frames for organizing knowledge about the world that we have inherited from the nineteenth century, we can begin to think more critically about the culture concept itself, how it is that we believe the world to be divided up into different cultures, and what the implications of that belief might be. No anthropologist that I have heard of wants to say there is no such thing as "culture" but since the 1980s many have been willing to say that the concept as anthropologists understand it is much fuzzier than what the rest of us (including historians) take it to mean. Too often, "culture" has come to stand for the way people who are not us do things. At its most reductive, this view doesn't allow for choice, rejection, resistance, ambivalence, and the whole range of options with which we credit ourselves. To that degree, it is deterministic: culture is what makes people do what they do. Culture itself does not change. In the new framework that many anthropologists employ, the term "cultural formation" replaces "culture" altogether, suggesting that change and adaptation are much more at the center of what we ought to be studying. One important instigator of change, of course, is encounter with another group of people.[12] In that context, the study of power and power relations are at the heart of the inquiry. The study of culture and cultural formations, then, leads into studies of everyday life. These studies bring to the surface the importance of looking at strategies apparently powerless peoples have used to maximize their chances of success in a world skewed against them. The development of the export market for art products in Meiji Japan provides an excellent example of the process.

In the period after Admiral Perry landed in Tokyo Bay and "opened" Japan to foreign trade, people in the United States, especially along the east coast, fell victim to an intense craze for things Japanese. Here was what looked like a true case of a culture doomed to quick extinction by exposure to the modernizing forces of the West. There was a flood of books about Japan in the United States, a flood of imports, and a flood of homemade products that looked Japanese. One of the early Western historians to study Japan even noted in 1905 that so prolific was the outpouring of books on Japan that "*not to have written a book about Japan is fast becoming a title to distinction.*"[13] In organization and structure, did this craze signal anything similar to the enthusiasm for African art with which it was nearly contemporaneous? This was the question I asked in preparing materials for teaching about Tokyo. In brief, was there organization on the Japanese side?

In a diary entry written by a Hartford resident who was visiting Tokyo in 1910 there appears a reference to a curio shop where funny practices were apparently going on. Reverend James Bulter-McCook, the tourist, records that the sellers were aging bronze objects artificially in order to be able to sell them as antiques. Who were the buyers, foreign tourists or Japanese? There is a body of anthropological literature on Japan that explores the phenomenon of conscious cultural formation, or the invention of tradition, as Japanese leaders sought to rectify the excesses of enthusiasm for things Western in Japan; but I was more immediately interested in looking at how Japanese viewed the foreigner's interest in things that were thought to embody truths about Japanese culture.

Reverend McCook brought home an extensive collection of objects bought in Japan, and added to his collection with things he purchased from dealers in Hartford. These objects are housed and on view in the house museum willed to the city when the last McCook died. The Japanese collection is maintained as McCook had arranged it, and it includes samurai suits of armor, helmets, sword hilts, large and small brass vessels, and porcelain and wooden objects. When these objects were appraised after the city had assumed possession of the house, they turned out not to be of great value; most of them were dated to the Meiji period.[14]

Meiji-period objects have only quite recently become collectors' items and hence have only recently begun to be studied. Previously, they played a poor second in the art market to objects having the stamp of authenticity.

"Authentic" objects, whether from Japan, India, West Africa, or wherever, are those thought to have been made before contact with Europeans. Postcontact objects are regarded by the arbiters of value in the West as fakes, hybrids, derivatives, or tourist art: in any case, nothing of value.

As Meiji pieces have become better known in art circles, material has been written about them that makes them accessible for teaching.[15] I have combined information on Meiji art production with materials on modernization during the Meiji period to make some of the same points in the world survey that can be made through the materials on the West African art trade.

In West Africa, the traders themselves seem to have been responsible for creating the market within West Africa and for contributing to the inclusion of West African objects in the world art market. In Japan, by contrast, government officials seem to have been the instigators. Even before the Meiji Restoration in 1868, leading daimyo (feudal lords) sent artisans abroad to international fairs and expositions with the purpose of learning about both foreign taste and processes of production. After 1868 and the abolition of Japanese feudalism and the daimyo status, the centralized government continued to send craftspeople and artisans abroad on information-gathering junkets. World's fairs were major destinations for these emissaries of commerce. Upon their return home, the information they supplied was used to set up government-run workshops to produce for the foreign market. The government also organized national expositions where craftspeople from around the country could learn the new techniques imported from the West. Many of the objects that found their way into Reverend McCook's house would have been produced in such government-sponsored workshops.

McCook gives some indication that he was aware of the Japanese production side. In his diary he comments: "More shops. At one, bronze things kept piled in water, full of water, drenched with water. Guide smiles as I suggest—'to make them green and old!'"[16] At another point in the diary he writes to a Japanese merchant in Yokohama asking him to find "the best specimens at the lowest price. . . . nothing that is not really good of its kind. Nothing modern." What McCook wanted, we might say, was to satisfy his nostalgic longing for a preindustrial past. "It is ironic," says art historian William Hosley, "that Japan emerged as a symbol of Western antimodernism at the same time she was exchanging her traditions for modernization. The 'Japan Craze' of the 1870s and 1880s was fueled by misperceptions and nostalgia. Part of what made Japan's modernization possible was its success in catering to the West's desire for art, consumer goods, and symbols of its premodern culture. By means created by modernization Japan was able to sell the idea of its traditional culture to the West and in so doing gain status and power among Western nations."[17]

Meiji period objects are variable, some looking like art nouveau productions and some, clearly, reproductions of older Japanese and Chinese
styles. It apparently did not take artists and artisans long to discover that
foreigners were not looking for anything modern from Japan, but wanted the
look of the old and traditional. In 1876 Japanese craftspeople were ready to
contribute significantly to the Philadelphia World's Fair, and the Japanese
pavilion at the fair was decidedly traditional. Japanese were already shopping
in Parisian-style department stores, cutting their hair in Western style, dressing in Western-cut clothing, and building houses that looked like houses in
the West, but for the Philadelphia fair their craftspeople built a traditional tea
house and offered for sale newly made reproductions of old objects.

This was the time when the Japanese government invited a bevy of foreign advisors, many of them American, to set up modern university departments in history, architecture, philosophy, and agriculture.[18] One of the advisors who came to teach philosophy, Ernest Fenellosa, was a recent Harvard
graduate who became interested in what he considered to be traditional Japanese art. Like sympathizers with the art revivalist cause in India, Fenellosa was
horrified by what he saw around him as the rush toward espousal of everything Western; and he urged his Japanese students to return to their cultural
traditions. One of Fenellosa's followers, Okakura, led a pan-Asian cultural revival movement, which aimed at binding together India, China, and Japan in
a united front against cultural encroachments from the West.

As I am suggesting, the cultural picture is extremely complex, and I have
not tried to unravel the whole of it in world history surveys. What has worked
for Meiji Japan is a dramatic role play meant to take place in a curio shop in
Tokyo at the time when Reverend McCook and his daughter were visiting. We
get some sense of what a curio shop might have looked like from a photograph
made by the first Western photographer to reach Japan, Felice Beato. I have
used Beato's photograph and description to re-create the curio shop. "Nothing attracts a stranger so readily as the sight of a Japanese Curio Shop," Beato
wrote. "The ingenuity and cleverness displayed in the manufacture of the exquisite little articles of ivory carving, cabinets, lacquered-ware, bamboo and
straw work, paper crockery, egg-shell china, etc., are admirable."[19]

McCook had perhaps spent many hours in these curio shops, or else
bought from dealers who did, since his house contains many of the items
Beato listed. I photographed these objects and had the photographs laminated so that the less fragile pictures could be used in place of the objects
themselves to furnish the shop. I then used a variety of secondary and primary sources to create the roles for people coming into the shop. 1910 turned
out to be a good year, full of cultural debate and controversy. Into the shop
come a variety of writers and artists, politicians, cultural conservatives and
Westernizers, craftspeople, and some older Tokyo residents (these entirely

fictional) hoping to sell off their old samurai heirlooms in order to make ends meet.

To reiterate, the scholarship that first alerted me to the importance of the international art market for understanding cultural exchanges in the nineteenth century was focused on the study of objects from West Africa. I employed insights from that study to the Japanese situation and found significant differences and some surprising similarities. Rather than being passive players in a Western-directed drama, both West African and Japanese merchants, manufacturers, and craftspeople played significant parts in setting the terms under which goods would be exchanged.

Conclusion: "We Have Met the Enemy and He Is Us"

One of the aims of studying other cultures, we have been told, is to learn more about ourselves. At the beginning of the twenty-first century, in a large body of scholarship that I have had in mind here, we seem to be facing a new dilemma: how, in studying other cultures, will we learn about anything other than ourselves? How can we actually learn about the past of places around the world if we, as Westerners, in some essential ways invented those pasts? Moreover, how can we learn about the "authentic" past if the very people who live there cooperate with our scenarios to keep us ignorant?

I have attempted to suggest that the questions are worth asking, of ourselves and our students, because those homegrown inventions are what we carry around with us. They needn't be all we take into the future, however. Through the process of becoming more aware of the range of our underlying assumptions and questioning why we have them, we begin to learn about our social selves, the selves that embody those traces left on us by history. It is when we, as teachers, begin to glimpse ourselves as products of history, with great potential but also with limitations imposed by who we are, where we live, what language we speak, that we will be able to help our students make their own entrance into the world.

Being skeptical about the uncritical use of the primary source; introducing the present of places we study; approaching the study of the precontact past with insights derived from the study of colonialism; exploring meaning making in the contact zone; and being willing to look comparatively at world areas we were taught to think were culturally separate can all be useful ways for teachers to position themselves as inquirers, open to the questions today's scholars of world areas, of colonialism, and of global culture are asking. None of these approaches, of course, is a panacea able to do away with all the problems associated with Eurocentric dominance. Nor can teachers apꞏch the immediate teaching of world history with an agenda that calls for them to have mastered twenty years of scholarship before they set foot in the classroom. What we want is not the answers, but the questions. Where better to start than with an awareness of what the recipients of Eurocentric dominance have been thinking about and doing all these years?

Notes

1. Quoted in Edward Said, *Orientalism* (New York: Vintage Books, 1979) 25.

2. See James Blaut, *The Colonizer's View of the World: Geographical Diffusion and Eurocentric History* (New York: Guilford Press, 1993).

3. See, for example, Ariel Dorfman and Armand Mattelart, *How to Read Donald Duck: Imperialist Ideology in the Disney Comic* (New York: International General, 1971).

4. The painter is the early twentieth-century Bengali painter, Jamini Roy. See Lou Ratté, "Sahridaya: Artist and Audience in Modern Bengali Art," in Clinton B. Seely, ed., *Calcutta, Bangladesh and Bengal Studies* (East Lansing: Asian Studies Center, Michigan State University, 1991), 29–44.

5. See, for instance, any of the issues of *Lalit Kala Contemporary*, the journal of the Indian Academy of Arts, in the 1970s and 1980s. Criticism in the journal raises issues about derivitiveness, cultural alienation, ambivalence toward Western influence, and the invention of tradition.

6. *The Cosmic Dancer: Shiva Nataraja,* an "Objects in Context" series exhibition (New York: The Asia Society Galleries, 1992).

7. Information on Queen Sembiyan Mahadevi is from Vidya Dehejie, *Art of the Imperial Cholas* (New York: Columbia University Press, 1990).

8. See Walter Benjamin, "The Work of Art in the Age of Mechanical Reproduction," in *Illuminations* (New York: Schocken, 1996), 217–51.

9. See Arjun Appadurai, ed., *The Social Life of Things* (Cambridge: Cambridge University Press, 1997), and Christopher Steiner, *African Art in Transit* (Cambridge: Cambridge University Press, 1995).

10. Steiner, 13

11. Steiner, No. 15, 166.

12. See Chapter One, "World History: Not Your Ordinary Survey," by Robert Andrian, above.

13. Basil Hall Chamberlain, *Things Japanese* (London: Kelley and Walsh, Ltd., 1905), 64.

14. Information supplied by Karen Peterson, curator of the Butler-McCook House, Hartford, CT.

15. I collected several booklets and articles describing Meiji art at the Asian Art Fair at the Armory in New York in 1998.

16. Diary of Reverend James McCook, Monday, June 1, 1908–Monday, June 15, 1908. Property of Butler-McCook House, Hartford, CT.

17. William Hosley, *The Japan Idea* (Hartford: Wadsworth Athenaeum, 1990).

18. See Stefan Tanaka, *Japan's Orient: Renderning Pasts into History* (Berkeley: University of California Press, 1993); John Maki, *William Smith Clark: A Yankee in Hokkaido* (Sapporo: Hokkaido University Press, 1996); *Japan: An Illustrated Encyclopedia*, vols. 1 & 2 (Otowa: Kodansha, 1993).

19. Felice Beato (attributed), Photographs of Japan, vol. II, 3-MQWST, New York Public Library, #99050-24-(61). Text accompanying a photograph titled "The Curio Shop."

5

World History Teaching
Where Do We Go from Here?

ROBERT K. ANDRIAN

Beyond the Banquet

Walladah Bint Al-Mustakfi was an eleventh-century Andalusian poet, a highly independent and individualistic woman, native to the city of Cordoba and daughter of its caliph. Not much biographical information exists on this remarkable woman, but we do know that she never married and that her house became *the* place to be for scholars, artists, and poets who were in search of both magnificent parties and brilliant intellectual discourse.[1] Thus Walladah's fame and cultural sophistication make her a perfect hostess for our *Medieval Banquet in the Alhambra Palace,* a gathering of invited guests from among the literati around the Eastern Hemisphere and primarily the Islamic Empire. I briefly introduced this learning experience in Chapter 1, but looking at this extravaganza more closely can help world history teachers continue to think about what students should know and understand in their courses. Moreover, focusing on the banquet as a teaching tool can lead teachers to think more about their conceptualizations of world history and the pedagogy accompanying these models.

While the banquet guests find their hearts touched by the exchanges of romantic poetical entreaties between Walladah and her boyfriend, the eleventh-century Cordoban court poet Ibn Zaydun, they are more intrigued by whom they meet at the banquet and, when Walladah invites a few special guests to speak to the entire group, by how much they may have in common with each other. The Cordoban Muslim physician and philosopher Ibn Rushd, who sought to prove that no conflict existed between faith and reason, indeed that there was a symbiotic relationship between science and religion, had been dead for more than twenty-five years before St. Thomas Aquinas was even born. Though they never met—except at this banquet—the Christian Aquinas referred to Ibn Rushd as the "Commentator," because the latter wrote a great deal about Aristotle. Aquinas quoted his Muslim counterpart over and over in an attempt to argue that reason and science were not enemies of Christianity, thus promoting a climate that would allow the Renaissance to spread from Spain to the rest of Europe. In the fourteenth-century fresco *St. Thomas Aquinas Enthroned* in the Santa Maria de Novella in Florence, Aquinas is pictured holding a book of wisdom that points to a human figure—none other than Ibn Rushd—in the center of the painting.[2] Surely Johannes Gutenberg never encountered the eleventh-century Song dynasty inventor of movable type, Pi Sheng, but he, like so many of his fifteenth-century European contemporaries, knew well of Chinese paper money, the magnetic compass, and gunpowder, among other Chinese inventions. The precursor of the renowned "Renaissance man," Leonardo da Vinci, may well have been the ninth-century Baghdad musician and scholar Abbas Ibn Firnas, whose ideas surrounding mathematics and science and music anticipated many of da Vinci's some six hundred years earlier. Firnas was recruited to teach in Cordoba, by far the largest city in Europe in the tenth century, with a population of 400,000—Paris, by contrast, had 40,000—containing among other things, seventy libraries with over a million volumes. The famed librarian Fatima traveled widely to places such as Cairo, Damascus, Baghdad, Samarkand, and Constantinople to acquire books for her libraries at Cordoba. The works were translated into Arabic and Latin and written on paper made there since 800. The ninth-century Baghdad Queen Zubaidah might not have been pleased to lose Abbas Ibn Firnas to the competing intellectual center of Cordoba in the Arab-Islamic Empire, but she enjoyed meeting the acclaimed Ar-Razi, chief physician of the Muslims, perusing Ibn Sina's medical text, one of 250 books the prodigious scholar wrote—as a child he had memorized the Qur'an by the age of ten—and listening to the stories of the inimitable world traveler during the days of the Pax Mongolia, the Moroccan Ibn Battuta. Like Baghdad's "House of Wisdom," Cordoba attempted to bring together all knowledge in the world.

On one level, teachers of world history would want to use the *Medieval Banquet in the Alhambra Palace* to illustrate the splendor of Arab-Islamic civilization. But there is larger significance to having students participate in this interdisciplinary extravaganza. We want them to know that discrete cultural regions did interact with each other in premodern times, in this case, in Dar al-Islam the "House of Islam" (see Figure 5–1). The view of Islamic civilization being restricted to the boundaries of the Middle East gives way to a broader, deeper meaning of a civilization that cuts across many cultural re-

Figure 5–1. *African expert Leo Africanus (left) enjoys a moment with Ibn Rushd (center) and St. Thomas Aquinas (right) at the banquet*
Photo by Wayne Dombkowski

gions and that embraces many diverse peoples, united in one sense, by the lingua franca of Arabic. As teachers we want to ask what Edward Said asks:

> Can one divide human reality, as indeed human reality seems to be genuinely divided, into clearly different cultures, histories, traditions, societies, even races, and survive the consequences? . . . For such divisions are generalities whose use historically and actually has been to press the importance of the distinctions between some men and some other men. . . . The result is usually to polarize the distinction—the Oriental becomes more Oriental, the Westerner more Western—and limit the human encounter between different cultures, traditions and societies.[3]

Ultimately I believe we would like our students of world history to begin to recognize, along with the historian Ross Dunn, "that the histories of particular peoples have always been embedded in contexts of human interaction that extend beyond their cultural boundaries. The 'culture' as an independent historical world is a delusion."[4] This understanding does not and should not deny the value of learning about particular societies and their traditions; it does, however, stress the reality that societies change over time and multiple cultural identities can emerge precisely because of cross-cultural encounters. Thus, our thinking about what students need to know about world history should be rooted right away in this bigger understanding of the essence of what world history is about.

Figure 5–2. *At the siege of Granada, the Inquisitor General Torquemada (center, in robe)*
presides over the book burning as Inquisition guards look on
Photo by Wayne Dombkowski

A delightfully entertaining and humorous play follows the dinner portion of the banquet at the Alhambra. Usually one class is assigned the responsibility of the performance, and the players do not disappoint their audience. Near the end of the play, a horse—the students make the costume, and usually two reluctant volunteers assume the role of the horse—comes to the rescue, and the forces of good once again triumph over evil, a predominant theme in many Arab folktales. But, much to the actors' chagrin, the play is rudely interrupted by the appearance of the Inquisitor General Tomás de Torquemada and his guards, and King Ferdinand and Queen Isabella, who have arrived to complete the siege of Granada in 1492 and the Christian Reconquest of al-Andalus from the Muslims. The Inquisition guards proceed to gather from the very startled Fatima precious books and manuscripts, including ornate and exquisite copies of the Qur'an and many mathematical and scientific texts, which guests have brought to the banquet to present as gifts to the hostess, Walladah. The Inquisitor well knows that a public book burning will break the hearts of the infidels (see Figure 5–2). As the flames rise, he orders the expulsion of the Sephardic Jews from Spain and the forced conversion of the Muslims; those who do not convert must also leave Spain. Cultural acceptance of diversity yields to bigotry, persecution, and conflict. I can safely add that the moment is not lost upon our students.

But where did the Jewish diaspora take these Sephardic Jews and their customs, their music, and their talents? We discover them at the eastern end of the Mediterranean living peacefully as part of the Ottoman empire, an empire that only a half century before the fall of Granada captured the city of Constantinople, thereby fueling the fire of the Christian Reconquest. Unlike the Christians, however, the Turks tolerated the Jewish faith and allowed the Jews to flourish professionally—even if they had to pay a special poll tax—enhancing the well-being of their own communities and of the empire itself. Skip ahead in time to the 1990s and the Serbian ethnic cleansing of Muslims in Bosnia, formerly part of the Ottoman empire until World War I. The Serbs, seeking to rebuild the Church and reclaim the land lost to the Ottomans, seem oblivious to the lessons of fifteenth-century history: "The cause of Islam and Turkey flourished [then] because so many Christians thought and behaved with the same suicidal intolerance . . . [displayed] today."[5] And we must also wonder today what has happened to Muslim tolerance of others' beliefs. Clearly students have much more history to learn before they can truly contextualize events and make thoughtful judgments in response to these kinds of analogous historical situations. But the message to world history teachers is clear. If we are committed to preparing our students to become global citizens, it is important to help them begin to make connections between "then" and "now." Asking students to find contemporary articles in the *New York Times*, for example, and then to write a reflection about how these articles relate to what the students have been studying in world history can enhance the process.

It's a Small World, After All

If today's students are to be able to understand and address the problems of an interdependent world and to become informed enough as citizens to make global decisions, they must first understand that the history of human experience has been one of profound and meaningful interconnection. Connections across societies over time—not just in this century of Americanization, not just in the last two centuries of Westernization, but throughout human history—help us to understand who we are, how we got that way, and where we are going. This understanding did not escape Wang Li, a fourteenth-century Chinese, when he reflected on the Mongol age:

> By the time of [Kubilai Khan] the land within the Four Seas had become the territory of one family, civilization had spread everywhere, and no more barriers existed. For people in search of fame and wealth in north and south, a journey of a thousand *li* was like a trip next door, while a journey of ten thousand *li* constituted just a neighborly jaunt. . . . Brotherhood among peoples has certainly reached a new plane.[6]

Globalization is among us and here to stay in a world of sovereign nation-states. While globalization has surely contributed to world economic growth and stability, as protesters from all over the world made clear in Seattle at the World Trade Organization meetings, globalization also brings with it significant tensions surrounding issues of wealth and poverty, human rights, environmental preservation, business and ethics, technology, gender inequality, public health and disease, and population growth. All of these issues tend to make cultural boundaries very fuzzy. And they mirror a number of universal historical themes that have shaped human history. These include:

- manipulating and changing the physical environment;
- developing tools and technology;
- peopling the globe;
- diffusing and exchanging ideas, tools, and other facets of culture;
- ending old frontiers and developing new ones; and
- creating increasingly more complex systems of politics, economics, and social interactions.[7]

World history conceptualizations need to focus on these themes so that students can better understand how their own histories and identities have evolved over time and space in an interconnected world history. They can begin to fit their own local and national experiences into larger global experiences. They may begin to see common values among civilizations that transcend cultural and political boundaries. Rather than imagining cultural diversity or pluralism as a threat as did Tomás de Torquemada or the ethnic cleansers of the '90s, they might, like Wang Li or Ibn Rushd, envision diversity as fundamental to the well-being and continued growth of individual societies and the global community.

Certainly the United Nations seems committed to managing globalization and enhancing its benefits for all. The General Assembly proclaimed the year 2000 as the International Year for the Culture of Peace and 2001 as the United Nations Year of Dialogue Among Civilizations. In direct contrast to those who view the violence and conflict of the post–Cold War era as part of a "clash of civilizations" paradigm of international relations—in particular, between Islam and the West—the UN proposes a paradigm of world politics based on inclusion rather than exclusion. Thus, the dialogue among civilizations will be between those "that perceive diversity as a threat and those that perceive diversity as an inherent element of growth and betterment."[8] Today's students of world history need to understand that throughout world history the outcomes of various cultural encounters have had much to do with this "dialogue" or lack thereof over the significance of diversity. Perhaps one of the many lessons we and they can learn from investigating these encounters, both contemporary and historical, is that human beings must care for one another. Nelson Mandela puts it well:

> As the possibility of nations to become islands sufficient unto themselves diminishes and vanishes forever, so will it be that suffering of the one shall at the same time inflict pain upon the other . . . What we speak of is the evolution of the objective world, which inexorably says to all of us that we are human together or nothing at all.[9]

Seven hundred years earlier, the Persian poet Sa'di offered the same injunction:

> The sons of men are members in a body whole related,
>   For of a single essence are they and all created.
> When Fortune persecutes with pain one member sorely, surely
>   The other members of the body cannot stand securely.
> O you from another's trouble turn aside your view
>   It is not fitting they bestow the name of "Man" on you.[10]

For the sake of having our students become more thoughtful about a twenty-first century, which will belong to *world* politics, economics, and culture, we need to construct our world history courses rooted in the investigation of human interconnection over time.

Envisioning a Model World History Curriculum

Most world history scholars would agree on the need for this kind of curriculum. Ross Dunn has suggested a number of conceptualizations for a world history survey that teachers ought *not* to teach. These "mythical" conceptions of world history include the following:

- world history as humankind's preparation for the Second Coming of Christ
- world history as the unfolding of freedom in Western Civilization
- world history as background information for simply studying current events
- world history as the study of different ancient and modern cultures
- world history as the stuff in the curriculum that's not about the United States[11]

The first conception provides us with a parochial linear history of Christianity running from the birth of Christ to the Final Judgment Day. The second essentially denies the rest of the world's peoples their histories or, as Lou Ratté intimates in Chapter 4, that we in the West have invented other peoples' pasts for them. This world history conception argues that students should wrestle with the question of the origins of our liberty today. It is American history pushed back through time beginning in East Africa, moving to Mesopotamia and Egypt, on to Greece and Rome, then medieval Europe—especially the Renaissance and Scientific Revolution—and finally across the Atlantic to the United States. African history in this view appears in the first chapter of the textbook but then disappears until slavery, the slave trade, and later European imperialism and colonialism. Dunn's third conception to be avoided by teachers, world history as background for studying current events, does not teach students in any depth about the study of history precisely because the focus is on contemporary affairs. Students are left without the necessary habits of mind to make sophisticated judgments about the challenges of their own world. A course for twelfth graders that addressed the question of why there is so much poverty in the world today could only be worthwhile if students had an in-depth world-historical foundation from which they could begin to contextualize the events of the present. The fourth model, emerging from the multiculturalism of the 1970s, brings us back to Edward Said's admonition against treating cultures as discrete entities. The study of Egypt and Mesopotamia, East Asia, South Asia, Mesoamerica, Sub-Saharan Africa, and various other regions of the world as separate units omits the connections among the regions. Students get exposed to the "civilization of the month" and usually to only the ruling classes of those civilizations. Once we get to the year 1500, the focus shifts to Europe, and students discover that things really begin to happen in the world. Finally, the fifth model separates U.S. History from world history, distorting the teaching of both. Is it conceivable that American history was never really a part of world history?

Thus, as Dunn suggests, we are left with the conceptualization of world history that makes the most sense; namely, world history as the "evolution of global processes and contacts, the interaction of societies, the nature of change in international frameworks, and comparisons among major societies."[12] In this conception the world is a biosphere inhabited by all of the human species, who all have histories, separate and intertwined. In this context, we as teachers want to ask what are the developments that our students ought to come to know and understand. If we want our students to consider the period from 1000–1500 as a vital one in understanding how the world was becoming a "smaller" place, rather than ask what was happening in 1450 in various civilizations around the world, we need to ask such questions as, who and what were responsible for all of the cross-cultural contact and exchange of goods and ideas, and how did these migrations and encounters affect peoples' lives and the societies in which they lived? If we want students to address key developments in the transatlantic slave trade during the period from 1500 to 1800, rather than ask what was happening in Europe, Africa, North America, and South America during that time, we might ask why did more Africans than Europeans migrate to the Americas between 1500 and 1800, and with what consequences to societies situated around the Atlantic rim?[13] The unit on the Atlantic slave trade, and the impact of migration patterns in the Americas described in Chapter 1, attempts to wrestle with these and other related questions.

I am not proposing anything terribly new here in terms of commitments teachers ought to be making to the study of world history. In many respects the Advanced Placement World History curriculum, which has been assembled by some of the top scholars and schoolteachers in the field, has adopted the conceptualization we have been affirming. Later in this chapter, I offer some thoughts about this new course, but right now I want to point out how the National Standards for World History reinforces an interactive global community model for the teaching of world history.

One of the main criticisms of the Standards when they appeared a few years ago was that too much Western civilization was missing. But to understand the Standards as a bible to inform teachers as to what to include and exclude in their world history courses is to misunderstand the purpose of the Standards.

The Standards divide human history into eight eras, from Paleolithic to present day. Each era comes with a set of large understandings, which students should grasp along with the development of critical thinking skills. Thus the Standards are meant to be guidelines for teachers as they conceive of the undergirding principles that will form the bedrock of their courses in world history. Students will come away with a more sophisticated understanding of the importance of European civilization and the concept of Westernization in the last five hundred years because, as the Standards assert, the teaching of any civilization will be enriched by placing that civilization in a larger historical context. Is it possible to suggest that Europe's development, indeed, its modernity, has been impacted by its contact with Africa, Asia, and the Americas and not simply from within its own borders? If not, then perhaps James Blaut is correct when he argues that those who believe that Europe "was more advanced and more progressive than all other regions (of the world) prior to 1492," also believe that its economic and social modernization must be fundamentally European, and that "therefore: colonialism cannot have been really important for Europe's modernization."[14] We will pursue this matter when we look at what students might come to know and understand about the Industrial Revolution.

While the Standards do not deny in any sense the importance of individual societies' traditions and histories, they emphasize the significance of crossing cultural boundaries in helping students begin to understand how and why human societies have changed over time. One Standard asks students to "assess ways in which the exchange of plants and animals between the Americas and Afro-Eurasia in the late fifteenth and the sixteenth centuries affected European, Asian, African, and American Indian societies and commerce."[15] Let's hear it for the Andean potato and the Iberian horse! Another Standard calls on students to "demonstrate understanding of how interregional communication and trade led to intensified cultural exchanges among diverse peoples of Eurasia and Africa" during the period from 1000–1500.[16] This Standard invites teachers to develop curricula that address not only the significance of the Mongol Empire and the hemispheric role of the Black Death, but also the exploits of travelers and adventurers such as Marco Polo, Ibn Battuta, Zheng He, and Prince Henry the Navigator, all of whom were at our banquet at the Alhambra. The National Standards, in reaffirming our conceptualization of an integrated world history, also encourage teachers to think about how they want students to talk about the world geographically at various junctures in world history.

World History's Geography

Dividing up the world's spaces, drawing boundaries, and representing the world as a whole on a map depend on the way we think about history, our own and that of others. The ancient Greek perception of the world imagined the Strait of Bosphorus as the demarcation of the boundaries of civilization. To the west of the strait, the "Western world" of the Mediterranean basin was civilized; to the east the world was different and inferior. World history geography has tended to mirror this dichotomy. Despite its geographic location clearly west of the Bosphorus, however, Africa has never been considered Western and thus "superior." Curiously, England and France, clearly part of Western civilization, while geographic neighbors, have had brutal histories of violent conflict, lending credence to Gandhi's memorable reply when asked what he thought of Western civilization: "I think it would be a good idea." Turkey, given the Ottoman-Islamic Empire, may be seen as alien to Europe, though Ataturk's Western reforms might suggest otherwise. Russia seems to become Western after Peter the Great, but lies east of the strait, and in the minds of western Europeans, continued to be excluded from the club.[17]

Is it really possible or even desirable to treat the "West" as a unit in terms of world history geography? Historical atlases have tended to do so with Euro-Atlantic-centered cartography but not without ideological peril. As Martin Lewis and Karen Wigen point out,

> The conventional cellular view of Eurasian historical geography—one that discerns only Europe, the Islamic world, India, and China, perceiving all other areas as merely the fuzzy edges of these great "civilizations"—evidently still does not have room for a complex and hybrid region like Southeast Asia.[18]

Part of the problem here, of course, is that the great "civilizations" approach to the study of world history found in many world history textbooks runs counter to a conceptualization rooted in cultural interaction. World history atlases tend to depend on this historical conception emphasizing in their maps European or Western civilization as the "greatest" of the major civilizations.[19] The cultural complexity of a region such as Southeast Asia cannot be understood by students unless they know of the immense contact over time between India and China and the Islamic world, and to a lesser extent between East Africa and places in Southeast Asia. Surely, for example, examining visual images in Cambodia—see *The World History Videodisc* listed in the appendix—can reveal both Hindu and Buddhist and later Islamic influences, and just as surely, listening to Vietnamese music can reveal the influence of Chinese instruments. Lewis and Wigen argue similarly when they critique cartographic depictions of eastern Asia:

> Paralleling the Eurocentricity of their overall conception, most historical atlases exhibit a secondary, but no less pronounced, Sinocentrism in their vision of East Asia. By focusing almost exclusively on the territorial extent of the Chinese empire under its various dynasties, historical cartographers implicitly reduce East Asia to the scale of a single country, whereas Europe is allowed to play the role of a culture area of continental scope. . . . the intimate connections between China and its closest cultural neighbors—Japan, Korea, Vietnam—are obscured. . . . Korea is simply ignored. . . . When it appears at all, Korea is reduced in the American historical-cartographic imagination to little more than a parade ground for foreign invaders.[20]

Then what about having our students focus on national labels rather than regions when they speak of the world geographically? After all, before the "invention" of Western civilization, before colonialism, Europe was exceedingly multicultural and multiracial. Even today European countries are full of such diversity in their cultural identities. Yet, the rise of nationalism in the last two centuries has made it difficult to portray empires with the geographic importance they deserve. National histories tend to lead to political geography with state boundaries that oversimplify cultural identities and focus on the impermeability of boundaries and the absence of frontiers. Students need to see the depiction, for example, of the Ottoman Empire from an Ottoman viewpoint, not from a strictly European one where it appears that Philip II of Spain is more concerned about the Dutch and the English than the Ottomans.[21]

If we as world history teachers are committed to an integrated world history, then we will want our world history geography to follow that commitment. Hence, representing the world geographically ought to stress the comparative relationships between states and regions and ought to focus on key periods of global exchange. The example of silver can help illustrate the point. While the flow of silver from Mexican mines to Spain helped to facilitate the rise of Spain as a world power in the sixteenth century, new scholarship demonstrates that the flow of silver illustrates trade that was truly global in nature and not just restricted to the Western Hemisphere, and certainly not limited in significance to the rise of Spain and by extension Europe. Dennis Flynn and Arturo Giraldez note that

> Throughout the seventeenth century, Pacific galleons carried two million pesos in silver annually (i.e., more than 50 tons) from Acapulco to Manila, whereupon it was quickly transshipped to China by Chinese merchants. . . . why does no one maintain that this Pacific drain of silver was caused by a dynamic Mexican demand for Asian products (in the face of stagnant Asian demand for Spanish-American output)?[22]

In the final analysis, most silver from the New World found its way to markets in Asia, particularly China. China imported huge amounts of silver from Japan as well. Later, in the eighteenth century even Europeans traded silver—not yet opium—to China across the Indian Ocean. Flynn and Giraldez go on to observe:

> The entire world economy was entangled in the global silver web. Millions of pesos in Peruvian silver were smuggled annually down the so-called "back door" of the Andes to the Atlantic ports of Buenos Aires and Sacramento during the Potosi silver cycle (1540s–1640s). This smuggled silver—eventually destined for the Chinese marketplace, of course—was exchanged for (smuggled) African slaves; evidently something far more complex than "triangular trade" was at work here.[23]

Thus, when we get students to speak about world history geographically, we need not only to have them understand the significance of cross-cultural exchange as a process that affects change in various societies, but also to understand its truly global nature. Cartographic representations will need to keep up with the commitment we make to conceptualize world history in unified ways.

Rethinking Conventional Narratives

In the final portion of this chapter I would first like to "reconsider" two major world-historical events, the Haitian Revolution and the Industrial Revolution, which I believe students should investigate. Second, I would like to offer a brief critique of the proposed Advanced Placement World History curriculum, which is presently being piloted by some secondary school teachers around the country.

Both the National Standards for World History and the AP World History syllabus have included in their periodizations of world history—in this case, the period from 1750–1914—guidelines for students to learn about the "Age of Revolutions," at least in the Western world. Eighteenth-century European Enlightenment thinking had begun to propel people to challenge the existing political and social order in the Atlantic Ocean system of empire. These challenges evolved into major revolutions in the Western Hemisphere: the American in British colonial North America, the French in France, the Haitian in the French Caribbean colony of Saint Domingue, and a number of Latin American revolutions in Central and South America. Teachers may decide to have students examine these revolutions comparatively and consider how preceding revolutions affected those that followed. A possible focus question might be: How and why did the rights of individuals and groups change as a result of these revolutions?

But I do believe that a thorough assessment of the Haitian Revolution is vital for students to undertake for a number of reasons. Through the slave trade, slavery, racism, and colonialism, and their effects on African slaves and their descendants, and through the subsequent impact of the success of the revolution on slaves and their masters elsewhere, the Haitian case study fits nicely into our overarching world history conceptualization of cultural diffusion and encounter. In analyzing the achievements of the slaves in Saint Domingue, the historian John Thornton introduces the important role that African—in this case, Kongolese—ideology may have had in the slaves' desire for freedom and success in gaining it.[24] The success of the Haitian Revolution, however, allows us to address some of the concerns Lou Ratté has put forward in Chapter 4. In selecting content for their students, world history teachers need to be conscious of how they can represent the latest scholarship in the field that continues to rethink ways of looking both at specialized regions of the world, and how peoples in these regions have interacted with each other. In particular, how can teachers ensure that the "lost voices" in world history, the "ordinary" people, the oppressed, the silenced, the "erased," the "marked," those heretofore left out of the history books, come to life in order that students can make more meaningful judgments about the course of events, and, in this case, the path to modernity?

In the case of the Haitian Revolution, the impact of outside influences, namely the American and French Revolutions, in particular the latter, on the success of Touissant L'Ouverture and his followers in Saint Domingue is unmistakable.[25] Yet, should we simply accept the notion that the idea of freedom was invented in the West? As Michel-Rolph Trouillot asserts, when assessing the historiography of the Haitian Revolution:

> The search for external influences on the Haitian Revolution provides a fascinating example of archival power at work, not because such influences are impossible but because of the way the same historians treat contrary evidence that displays the internal dynamic of the revolution. Thus, many historians are more willing to accept the idea that slaves could have been influenced by whites or free mulattos, with whom we know they had limited contacts, than they are willing to accept the idea that slaves could have convinced other slaves that they had a right to revolt.[26]

Haitian slaves did not rely on esoteric Enlightenment conceptions of freedom, nor on radical Jacobin ideology, nor on Creole versions of Kongolese royal claims; instead they presented demands to the French as early as 1791 that were rooted in indigenous peasant circumstances such as, according to Trouillot, "three days a week to work on their own gardens and the elimination of the whip. . . . Such evidence of an internal drive . . . is simply ignored, and this ignorance produces a silence of trivialization."[27] Part of the internal drive came as a response to the planters' prohibiting slaves from engaging in cultural activities such as dancing, drumming, and singing. These practices, closely allied to West African religious rituals and the theology of vodoun, served as inspiration for the slave revolution that began in 1791.

Even when the mass insurrection of 1791 occurred, the French could not conceive that black slaves could foment such a rebellion. When they did, the French believed they would easily suppress the slaves. As one delegate to the National Assembly, Jean-Pierre Brissot, explained: "What are 50,000 men, badly armed, undisciplined and used to fear when faced with 1,800 Frenchmen used to fearlessness?"[28] Precisely because the Haitian revolution successfully, at least for a moment, challenged Western colonialism, did the dominant powers attempt to erase the story from their memories, or continue to think it unthinkable. Many in the fledging American republic refused to accept Haitian independence. Thomas Jefferson called Touissant L'Ouverture and his followers "the cannibals of the Terrible Republic."[29] In 1801 as president, Jefferson informed French leader Napoleon Bonaparte that he "would be happy to supply a fleet to 'reduce Touissant to starvation.'"[30] Congressman Albert Gallatin in 1799 was unalterably opposed to an independent Haitian state:

> What is this population? It is known to consist, almost altogether, of slaves just emancipated, of men who received their first education under the lash of the whip, and who have been initiated to liberty only by the series of rapine, pillage, and massacre, that have laid waste and deluged that island to blood; of men, who if left to themselves, if altogether independent, are by no means likely to apply themselves to the peaceable cultivation of the country, but will try to continue to live, as heretofore, by plunder and depredations. . . . if left to govern themselves, they might become more troublesome to us, in our commerce to the West Indies . . . they might also become dangerous neighbors to the Southern States, and an asylum for renegades from those parts.[31]

Not surprisingly the United States did not recognize Haitian independence until one year before Lincoln's Emancipation Proclamation.

I would encourage teachers of world history to immerse their students in a thorough investigation of the Haitian Revolution. At the very least its study can convey to students the important notion that change in human society resulting from cultural encounter does not come from only those who have the power. Those who do not have power can challenge a number of elite groups . . . and win. Moreover, a consideration of the Haitian case in the "Age of Revolutions" challenges the dominant modernization paradigm, embedded as we noted earlier, in the world historical conceptualization of the march toward American liberty.

While we are on the subject of revolution, let's turn to the development of industrialization and the case of the Industrial Revolution. Conventional interpretations of the Industrial Revolution would have students understand that it was a swift and dramatic break with past economic patterns of development that began rather suddenly in England and rapidly spread to the European continent and North America. Technology paved the way for the exploitation of coal, which led to iron and steel production and increased productivity, which led to steam engines and railroads, which in turn led to industrial cities, which led to a modern economy, state, and society. The conventional interpretation fits neatly into a conceptualization of world history that tells the triumphalist story of Western material progress and that logically, according to the story, equates modern with Western. Expressive cultural development seems to be the province of the rest of the world, which, until it becomes "modern," will remain "traditional." But what our students need to know and understand about the Industrial Revolution is informed by more recent scholarship, which insists on placing the causes and effects of the Industrial Revolution in a larger global context that emphasizes the interconnectedness of a global economy.

We would want our students to be able to raise and wrestle with questions such as what were the global circumstances in the mid-eighteenth century that might have facilitated the emergence of substantial economic development? In what ways were these developments revolutionary, and in what ways, perhaps, were they evolutionary within the context of a world economy as a whole? How were the existence of English cotton colonies and the presence of slave labor in those colonies related to the development of English cotton mills? Both England and China had substantial coal deposits, so why did not industrialization occur in China as well? In what ways was the Industrial Revolution a global phenomenon, which profoundly affected the lives of peoples and nations over the course of time, in some cases in unexpected and uncontrollable ways? "Can the effects of major economic and technological change in any era be limited and controlled, or will these effects bring global consequences that go beyond the expected?"[32] What was the interrelationship between industry and empire and colonialism? Why did so many laborers migrate all over the world and where did they go? With this approach, we certainly accept the reality that certain remarkable developments did indeed occur in Lancashire, England, in the 1730s, but that the so-named Industrial Revolution was a long, gradual process that occurred within a well-established global economy and a mature Atlantic economy, of which England was one of many numerous players. This understanding helps reinforce the global perspective we want students to have from the outset of any world history course. It also allows them to engage in comparative studies within and among societies who became impacted by industrialization.

AP World History

The Advanced Placement World History course wants students to acquire certain habits of the mind, namely, to:

- see global patterns over time and space while also acquiring the ability to connect local developments to global ones and to move through levels of generalizations from the global to the particular
- develop the ability to compare within and among societies, including comparing societies' reactions to global processes
- develop the ability to assess claims of universal standards while remaining aware of human commonalities and differences; putting cul-

turally diverse values in historical context; not suspending judgment but developing understanding.[33]

These mind-sets are both ambitious and noble, and those who have worked so diligently to create the course syllabus, still a work in progress, have wisely adopted, in part, the conceptual model that we have been encouraging all along in this chapter. Rooted in the premise that cultural interaction has been the driving force behind change in human society—and, given the globalization of today's world, will continue to be such a force—this model shuns the notion of rigid and static cultural boundaries within and among societies in favor of uncertain and fluid frontiers. This model allows students to make meaningful comparisons about patterns of change—or lack thereof—among societies in response to developments, which can be globally contextualized. Thus, the course affords students the opportunity to a degree to become sophisticated students of history with a particular affinity for world-historical thinking.

The periodization of AP World History mirrors, with minor variations, that of the National Standards, assuming that one accepts the validity of the notion that the course "begins" its historical survey in the year 1000. While all chronological divisions are somewhat arbitrary and biased, teachers and students need these denotations of turning points and interrelated developments over periods of time to help make sense of the past. The AP historical periods are 1000–1450; 1450–1750; 1750–1914; and 1914–Present. The National Standards encourage teachers to have students learn about three additional historical periods prior to the year 1000, while the AP course in effect dehistoricizes these years, simply referring to them as the "Foundations" section of the course syllabus.[34] For each period on the suggested AP course syllabus, well-conceived overarching themes, habits of the mind, and overarching questions are listed. Guideline sources, both primary and secondary, have been suggested, and many teachers in the summer of 2000 began work on creating specific lesson plans complete with assessments and learning activities for each of the course's teaching units. Certainly the course will continue to be polished and refined over time, but the first AP Test in world history is scheduled to take place in May 2002.

That there is even a College Board mandate for AP World History says a great deal about the burgeoning nature of the discipline of world history in the last generation. Much good work on the part of both scholars and secondary school teachers—not that the two groups are mutually exclusive—has gone into the development of the AP World History course. While I may not concur with some content choices—I would periodize world history prior to 1000, for example—my primary concern with the course is pedagogical.

I worry that the course's one-year time frame will lead its teachers and their students to fall into the trap of trying to "cover" history, rather than "uncovering" it, as they move inexorably forward to the AP test date, a date that already shaves off a healthy amount of teaching time from a proposed thirty-six-week syllabus. I worry that, given time constraints, teachers will find it more difficult to make world history come alive for their students, and that consequently, students will be left with little time to actually "do" history and engage in much of the motivating activities which Mark Williams describes in Chapter 6. Would it be possible, still, to take that field trip to the Mashantucket Pequot museum to explore the cultural encounter of the Europeans and Native Americans? I worry that the proposed AP syllabus forces teachers away from the "less is more" principle of learning, leaving students with but a superficial understanding of peoples and societies and how they have interacted and changed over time. Will the syllabus allow for a case studies approach to provide an in-depth examination of the theme of cultural encounter? While case studies, as Philip Curtin observes, "can only be a partial reflection of the broader processes of history . . . they make it possible to stay closer to the empirical data on which all good history must be based."[35] Given the commitment on the part of AP teachers to get their students to be able to contextualize globally, to understand what is significant in world-historical terms, and ultimately to arrive at a sophisticated understanding of developments that occurred in the past, I worry that the one-year time frame for this course would result in achieving the exact opposite from what it intended.

Students might be forced to rely simply on textbook-driven learning, and despite, in the past few years, improvements in world history textbooks and all of the ancillary materials they contain, such sources often claim to be omniscient carriers of the historical truth. Will students have the time to think about how contemporary events in the world relate in some way to what they are studying about the past? In both world history courses at Loomis Chaffee, students are asked to read the *New York Times*, periodically select an article from the paper, and write a reflection that attempts to make some connection between past and present. Will students be able to consider, as Gilda Lerner so aptly wonders, when stressing the need for teachers to include a thorough examination of women and women's view of the world in world history: "What did women do while men were doing what the textbook tells us was important?"[36] I worry about opportunities for interdisciplinary study in this course. Would students be able to use, for example, the music and dance of West African vodoun to help investigate the mind-set of Haitian slaves during the revolution, or to address the question of whether or not African traditions were preserved as part of their involuntary migration? I worry about the issues Lou Ratté raises in Chapter 4 about our attitudes toward selecting content, about being able to get students to recognize the challenges scholars have in working with primary sources, about being able to wrestle, for example, with the idea that we, as Westerners, have, in part, "invented" others' pasts, so how can we *really* learn about them? Finally, I worry about making sure that we fulfill our ultimate mission as teachers of world history: to turn kids on to its study, and to make them lifelong learners. In the final analysis, they have to really *want* to read what we assign them to read.

Wherein lies the future of world history teaching? At Loomis Chaffee, we have a two-year history requirement in order for students to graduate. One year is a world history course about which you have read in Chapters 1 and 3. The other year is United States history. My proposal, radical as it might sound for an independent boarding school, is that we create a two-year world history course that incorporates U.S. History into world history. From the standpoint of world history and the primary global conceptualization of world history we have been discussing in this chapter, such a proposal is not radical sounding at all. Some schools already engage in such a "radical" curriculum. Others, who may have more than a two-year graduation requirement, ought to consider doing so.

I remember being astounded eight years ago while attending a World History Institute in Aspen, Colorado, when its leader, Heidi Roupp, one of the gurus in the field of world history, explained to me that she was teaching a *three-year* world history course at Aspen High School. Concerned American history teachers should follow the lead of African American scholars. As Robin Kelley writes:

> We have much to learn from African-American historical scholarship about the international context for American history. "Internationalizing" United States history is not about telling the story of foreign policy or foreign relations but about how tenuous boundaries, identities, and allegiances really are. . . . there is no United States history outside of world affairs.[37]

It would be hard to deny, would it not, the global connection of such revolutionary movements as the Easter Rebellion in Ireland, the Mexican Revolution, the Russian Revolution, and the Harlem Renaissance.

Working on a two-year world history course, which will incorporate many of the ideas we have talked about in this chapter and others in this book—surely we would have our Banquet at the Alhambra—presents an exciting opportunity for colleagues within the history department for both professional and curriculum development. But, creating such a curriculum also affords additional opportunities to bring in colleagues from outside the discipline—my wife, for example, teaches a World Music course at our school—and to collaborate with scholars from neighboring colleges and universities.

Such collective wisdom and experience in inspiring young minds offers yet another means to enhance our understanding of world history, what to teach and how to teach it. Perhaps in the future, such inspired students of world history will go on to pursue the field at the undergraduate and graduate levels, ultimately becoming teachers themselves.

Notes

1. Audrey Shabbas, ed. *A Medieval Banquet in the Alhambra Palace,* rev. ed. (Berkeley: AWAIR, 1993), 145.

2. *Encyclopedia of World Art,* vol. XIII, s.v. *St. Thomas Aquinas Enthroned Between the Doctors of the Old and New Testaments, with Personification of the Virtues, Science and Liberal Arts.* The artist, Andrea de Firenze, began the work in 1365 and completed it circa 1370.

3. Edward Said, *Orientalism: Western Representation of the Orient,* 45–46, quoted in Ross Dunn, *Western Civ, Multiculturalism, and the Problem of a Unified World History* (Springfield, VA: ERIC Reports, 1995), 7.

4. Dunn, *Unified World History,* 14.

5. Karen Meyer, "When Turks Saved the Jews," *New York Times,* 15 October 1995. The teacher can hand out the article after discussing the Banquet and let students process it.

6. Jerry Bentley, *Old World Encounters* (1993), 111, quoted in Dunn, *Unified World History,* 15.

7. Simone Arias, Marilynn Hitchens, and Heidi Roupp, "Teaching World History: The Global Human Experience Through Time," *ERIC Digest* (Bloomington, IN: ERIC Clearinghouse, April, 1998), 1.

8. Ruhollah Ramazani, "Some Thoughts on the Dialogue Among Civilizations" (Department of Government and Foreign Affairs, University of Virginia, Charlottesville, VA, June, 2000, photocopy), 1.

9. Ruhollah Ramazani, "The Blending of Civilizations?" *Middle East Insight* (July–August 1999): 19.

10. Ibid.

11. Ross Dunn, "A.P. World History" (paper presented at World History Association Summer Institute, San Francisco, CA, August 2000), 7.

12. Ibid., 8.

13. Ibid., 12.

14. James Blaut, *The Colonizer's Model of the World: Geographical Diffusionism and Eurocentric History* (New York: Guilford Press, 1993), 2.

15. *National Standards for World History: Exploring Paths to the Present* (1994), 172, quoted in Dunn, *Unified World History,* 10. The *U.S. News and World Report* six-page flyer titled, "The Indian Homeland" and "The Columbian

Exchange" functions as an effective teaching tool for students. Order from USN&WR Reprints, 2400 N. St., N.W., Washington, DC 20037.

16. *National Standards for World History*, 138, quoted in Dunn, *Unified World History*, 11.

17. Jack Goldstone, "Geography in World History" (paper presented at World History Association Summer Institute, San Francisco, CA, August 2000), 1.

18. Martin W. Lewis and Karen E. Wigen, *The Myth of Continents: A Critique of Metageography* (Berkeley: University of California Press, 1997), 130–32.

19. More recent atlases have begun to move beyond this conception. See, for example, Magellan Geographix, *World History Atlas* (Santa Barbara, CA, 2000). Magellan Geographix is the custom cartographic division of Maps.com. See http://www.maps.com.

20. Ibid.

21. Goldstone, "Geography in World History," 2.

22. Dennis Flynn and Arturo Giraldez, "Cycles of Silver: Global Economic Unity Through the Mid-18th Century," in *World History for the 21st Century*, vol. 3 (National Endowment for the Humanities and The College Board, photocopy), August 2000, 4.

23. Ibid., 8

24. John Thornton, "I Am the Subject of the King of Congo: African Political Ideology and the Haitian Revolution," *Journal of World History* 4, no. 2 (1993): 181–214.

25. See David Geggus, "The Haitian Revolution," in Franklin Knight and Colin Palmer, eds., *The Modern Caribbean* (Chapel Hill, NC: University of North Carolina Press, 1989), 26–31.

26. Michel-Rolph Truillot, *Silencing the Past: Power and the Production of History* (Boston: Beacon Press, 1995), 103.

27. Ibid., 104.

28. Ibid., 91.

29. "How Revolutionary Was the American Revolution? Haiti and American Slave Rebellions, 1791–1804" (World History Association Summer Institute, San Francisco, CA, photocopy), August 2000, 1.

30. Ibid., 2

31. Ibid.

32. Daniel Berman and Robert Rittner, *The Industrial Revolution: A Global Event*. National Center for History in the Schools (Los Angeles: UCLA, 1998), 5. See the simulations sections of the appendix for how to obtain any of the curriculum units published by the NCHS.

33. *Advanced Placement Course Description: World History* (Princeton, NJ: The College Board, September 2000), 7.

34. Ibid., 12.

35. Philip Curtin, *The World and the West: The European Challenge and the Overseas Response in the Age of Empire* (Cambridge: Cambridge University Press, 2000), xi.

36. Gilda Lerner, "Twelve Questions to Bring Women into View" (paper presented at the World History Association Conference, Colorado State Univ., June 1999), 1.

37. Robin D. G. Kelley, "'But a Local Phase of a World Problem': Black History's Global Vision, 1883–1950." *Journal of American History* 86 (December 1999): 1075–76.

6

If It's Dull, It's Not History

MARK WILLIAMS

In deliberations over what ought to happen in a world history course, one element that surely ranks in importance with content and process objectives is motivational strategy. Unfortunately, amidst the often heated discussions about "content standards" and the relative value of content as opposed to skills, the whole matter of how to get students excited enough to learn anything at all is often overlooked. Creating lifetime learners of history, or even schooltime learners, means that teachers need to engage students' imaginations, make the past come alive for them, show them that history is about real people, get them to initiate investigations, give them a sense of ownership of the subject matter, and treat them as though they were capable of sophisticated thinking.

In this chapter I discuss some of the techniques that I use to get kids hooked on history. I have no illusions that I provide a full compendium of motivational strategies here. Rather I hope to suggest a few principles for thinking about motivation that will, in the long run, inspire even more creative ideas to emerge from my audience. Furthermore, I want to offer the overarching thought that motivation amounts to far more than gimmickry or trickery, but involves fully attending to what we lovers of history know is true: history, by itself, is exciting. We are fully capable of making it dull, to be sure, but it doesn't have to be that way! In fact, I would go so far as to say that if it's dull, it's not history.

What Is It We Love?

Perhaps the best place to start is to give some thought to the question of just what it is about history that is exciting for us. As teachers of the subject, something must have grabbed us somewhere along the way. Sure, there are the rational forces at work. Like history teachers for at least a century we may be convinced that knowledge of history or skill in historical thinking makes better citizens, be they citizens of a democratic nation-state, or citizens of a global community. We may be of the opinion that practicing historical thinking is good survival training for people in all walks of life; or there may be among us a good number of democrats (with a small "d") who believe that history teaches us the route to freedom.

As true as these suppositions are, it is unlikely that they alone instilled in us a love of history—more likely they provide plausible arguments that a group of people who are doing what they love are still socially useful. Besides, how many sub-twenty-year-olds are deeply concerned about becoming good citizens, skillful decision makers, or freedom fighters? (sub-thirty-year-olds?) (I'll stop there before I appear cynical.)

No, we need to go beyond the rational to get at what's exciting about history. And I suppose that there are different aspects of the discipline's "affective" side that appeal to different people. Therefore, I am, to some extent, speaking for myself as a history lover here. But let's consider the document in Figure 6–1.

Now this is history.

The document is taken from the land records of the town of Simsbury, Connecticut, and is dated 1720. Looking at it alone, most people would be hard-pressed to see in it the embodiment of history's grip on the human imagination. This lack of sensitivity to all that is beautiful is excusable in this case, however, because we are not looking at the actual document, but rather at a black-and-white representation of it in a book about teaching world history. But imagine yourself in the Simsbury town vault hefting a twenty-pound volume out of a rack in a remote corner of the room. You place it on a table that you are sharing with five lawyers or paralegals hurriedly completing title searches on behalf of clients who are eager to develop the next subdivision. You open to a page of crinkled brown three-century-old paper covered with indecipherable scrawl, and you study it intently. Believe me, even if you have absolutely no plans to do anything with the document, it's worth the lifting just to see the lawyers' reactions.

Now, let's suppose you actually have some context for the document. You've been studying the tiny settlement of Salmon Brook in the northern reaches of Simsbury. You paid attention to this document because it

Ebenezar ⌞ 10 ⌟ Lamsons Land

Land im Simsbery belonging to Ebenezar Lamson Lying between the two
branches of Samon Brook a litle Distant from Crooked Brook also Lying
Easterly of a place Called brushey hill: began to messure att north wester-
ly corner at an ocke Stadle which had Stones Sett down by it from the
Dcc: Runne East and by South thirty Rods two Rods then went back to the
Said ocke and from thence turning the Square Southerly thirty Rod and put
Ched down Stones for the South west Corner then turned the Square any
Runne Easterly thirty two Rods: So Land is bounded Easterly and westerly
on the Commons North on Land belonging to Sam[ll] addams see South on
Land belonging to nathaniell holcomb jun[r] So Land was Granted to So Lamson
att a Town meeting of the Inhabetants of Sims bery Januarey the nine
teenth: 17 12/20 and on Coonditions as be Seen in the Record of the Grant in the
third Book of Town acts: fol: 15: and was Layd out and bounded aprieh 28th:
:1720 pr: John humphris Surueyer

Land in Simsbery belonging to Nathaniell holcomb: junr: being the third
nathaniell: So Land: is Lying within the Township of Sims bery Lying
westward of Samon Brook houses lying between the branches of Samon
Brook lying northerly of and alitle part on Crookid Brook began att north
East corner and Run South and by west down the Brook thirty two Rods
to awhile ock Stump then went back to the first So corner which is likewise
Lamsons South East corner and from thence by Lamsons Lyne Run west
twenty Rods Sett Stones then turned the Square and Run South and by west
thirty two Rods and Sett down Stones for the South west Corner this peice
Contaynes four accres then began fr a second peice to make up his Comple-
ment: began att awhite ock Stump which is likewise the South East corner
of the first peice and Run South and by west twenty two Rods and marke
a maple Tree Standing on South Sid of Crookid Brook then went back
to the first Butment and Runn west ward fifteen Rods Sett down a
Stone then turned the Square and runn South and by west twenty
two Rods Sett down a Stone by the Brook Called Crooked Brook this peile
Contaynes two accres So that both peices Contayne Six accres acording
to his grant which was granted to him at a Town meeting of the
Inhabetants of Sims bery: Januarey the nine teenth — 17 12/20 See 3d
Book of Town acts fol: 15: So Land is bounded north on Ebenezar
Lamsons lott the other Sids on the Commons: Laid out and bounded aprieh
:28th 1720 pr: John humphris Surueyer

Land in Simsbery belonging to George hayes junr: which Land was
granted to So hayes att a Town meeting of the Inhabetants of Sims bery
the ninteenth day of Januarey: 17 12/20 as may be Seen in the 3d Book of
Town acts: fol: 12: So Land is Scitate lying and being within the
Township of Simsbery westward of Samon Brook houses Lying East
ward of Crooked Brook between So Brook and the hopp yeard Lying on
the Sid of brushy hill: we began att the South west Corner att a
Cuple of black assh Trees markt and Sett down Stones by it and from
So Tree Runn an East point baring alitle to the north forty Rods
and made a heap of Stones: then turned the Square northward ly Six
teen Rods and made a heap of Stones then went back to the first butment
and from So assh Tree messured north Sixteen Rods: So Land is forty
Rods in length and Sixteen Rods in bredth and is by Estimation four
accres acording to his grant and is bounded forth on Land left for
ahigh way at the other Sids on the Comons: sett out and bounded the
twenty Eight daye of Aprieh 1720: pr John humphris Surueyer

Figure 6–1. From Simsbury land records—1720 grants

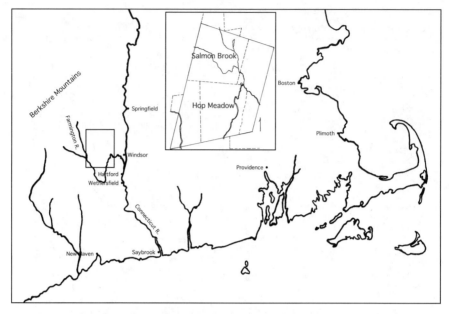

Figure 6–2. *Colonial Simsbury in New England (Inset: Salmon Brook in Simsbury)*

makes reference to lands that are near this settlement. In 1720 Simsbury lay on the northwestern edge of the English domain in New England (see map in Figure 6–2). Simsbury's residents were well aware of their precarious position, having been told by the colony's legislature during the last war with the French (1702–1713) that if they abandoned their homes in favor of the relative safety of one of the towns on the Connecticut River, they would forfeit their freeholds. In other words, they were being positioned on the western frontier of the colony to establish an English presence and to push the frontier outward. Even though the 1713 Peace of Utrecht had put a temporary stop to the conflict between France and England, the frontiers where their empires were grinding together still seethed with tension in the 1720s. As late as 1725 Simsbury's militiamen were being called up and sent west to the Housatonic River valley to ferret out Huron raiding parties.

That is the political and military context, but it is the particular social and geographic contexts that are even more interesting for viewing this old scrap of paper. In studying the town's land records in detail, I determined that the recipients of these land grants were all young men who lived with their families in the small collection of houses at Salmon Brook. This outlying village was the most exposed of Simsbury's, and of Connecticut's, settlements. First inhabited by English-speaking people in the 1680s, it was abandoned briefly during King William's War (1689–1697), and finally resettled permanently by the early 1700s.

Simple curiosity drove me to ask who these people were (I guess it had something to do with my living in the area), and it was the result of that search that made the 1720 land grants so interesting. After some investigation into Connecticut vital and probate records, court documents, and genealogies, it turns out that the original settlers of Salmon Brook, parents of the men who received the land grants in 1720, all had one thing in common, and it was not being English or Puritan, as one might expect of New England farmers. In fact, of the first ten family heads that inhabited the settlement, three were Welsh, one was a former Huguenot, and one was a Scot. Additionally, one was the son of a convicted witch, one was fleeing from creditors in Wethersfield, Connecticut, one had been an indentured servant in Windsor, and three had openly broken with the Puritan establishment and embraced the Church of England. Not surprisingly, none of them had been given free grants of land by the towns in which they lived before moving to Salmon Brook. Thus, the one thing that they all had in common was that they were people who were socially on the fringe of the Connecticut colony. We might be tempted to refer to them as "bottom-dwellers," or, at least, "outsiders."

The leaders of the colony and of Simsbury's parent town of Windsor were willing to give them land, but only very dangerous land. To appreciate how dangerous their situation was, one needs only to look at a map drawn about that time, another neat old scrap of paper to be found among Connecticut's colonial archives (see Figure 6–3). This drawing shows that the Salmon Brook houses were located northwest of Simsbury's "Great Fort," that is, militarily in front of the facility that had been erected to protect them! And

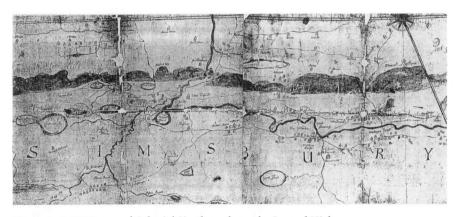

Figure 6–3. *1736 map of Colonial Simsbury drawn by Samuel Higley*

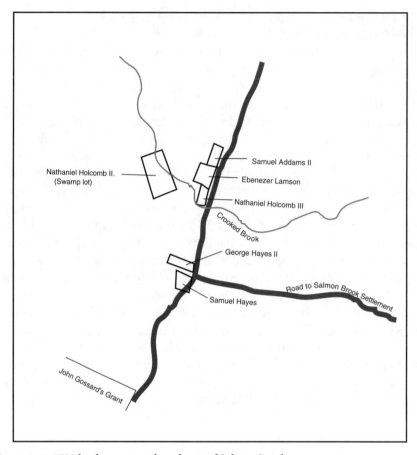

Figure 6–4. *1720 land grants north and west of Salmon Brook*

the 1720 grants to the children of Connecticut's fringe elements were even far-ther northwest from the first settlement (see Figure 6–4). Their beloved free-holds, which they were forbidden to abandon on pain of forfeiture, were nes-tled in a continental battlefield forward of their side's front lines!

I found the discovery of the social and geographic context of these 1720 land grants terrifically exciting. It revealed to me the manner in which the colonial elite did business: by pushing their "outsiders" into the no-man's-land with offers of free land. Thus, the English domain could be extended by occupation—occupation by a surly lot who would defend their land vehe-mently. Needless to say, these people were very adept at trapping wolves and wildcats, shooting crows by the dozen, and scalping Indians, all activities that earned them sizable bounties (which helped them pay off sizable debts for which they were periodically jailed). Consequently, the social context also revealed to me the continuing active role played by those outsiders as they impressed and pressured the elite to accommodate them with more free land for their maturing children. Here I was able to gain some important insight into the nature of Euro-American expansion and colonialism. The vanguards of the empires were not armies flanked by Indian guerrillas, but families—families of "outs," whose children would be rewarded for their parents' conquests with the land by which they would achieve the status of "ins."

What was most exciting, however, was the process of discovery itself. As I moved from one document to another in my search for these people whose names would never make it to a history text, I was slowly peeling back the gossamer layers covering the past of the community in which I lived, with each new view getting me closer to seeing what life was like three centuries ago. I was at the controls of that time machine all historians long to operate, my target subjects changing from dark shadows into real people. Or is it more appropriate to think of the process as working on a jigsaw puzzle? The brown crinkly scraps of paper were my oddly shaped pieces, each containing nothing but blotches of color. My skills as a decoder of such material were the hands fitting the puzzle pieces together. My imagination was my resort to complete the picture when I found that many of the puzzle pieces had been lost forever, a situation all historians must accept as fundamental to the nature of history.

I could now conjure up images of my farmers clearing their land of trees and predators, boarding up their windows at night, staring down town proprietors who were reluctant to give them too much land, riding off in their militia units on patrol, and planting their orchards and grain fields in anticipation of a bright and more secure future—and a future characterized, ironically, by the very autonomy the colonial elite was afraid to give to the "lower orders." Is not this process of discovery, this searching for long-hidden clues, this act of combined analysis and imagination what makes history exciting? And is that process not history itself? Then this is what must happen for our students.

Films and Field Trips

Showing films and taking students on trips are natural recourses for teachers who want to make history come to life. I certainly show my share of movies and contribute disproportionately to the disruption of my school by driving students off for whole days. Nevertheless, a note of caution is in order here. Too often teachers take refuge in the medium itself, be it a film or a trip, without considering either its teaching potential or its real motivational power.

Kids seem to like to watch a motion picture (at least they're quiet!), and a field trip is a nice break from the daily grind of sitting in classrooms and responding robotically to bells. But do they actually learn much staring at the screen for an hour? And do they really find what they are watching or touring all that exciting? Has history—real history—truly "come alive"?

I would argue that the answer to those questions is generally "no." There are a lot of fine educational films on the market, and in many cases a great deal of money has been put into their creation. Yet, for the most part, they amount to flashy lectures during which, because of darkness, students are relieved from taking notes. Similarly, there are a lot of museums and historical sites in our country, and many have full-time educational staffs hard at work developing programs for young people. Yet, again, when students visit, they usually play the role of listeners and lookers, not active learners. The captivating nature of the screen and the three-dimensional exhibits of a museum do not automatically translate into excitement about the history being represented. I have spoken with a good many frustrated teachers who recount how yawns and indifference are commonplace when they are showing a film, and inattention and socializing are the usual scene on field trips.

The reason, of course, is that historical films and sites are not history by themselves, and thus, they are not exciting simply because they are films and sites. It is what students bring to these activities that makes them exciting. That is, if a film or a trip is an integral part of the process of discovering the past, with the student as the discoverer actively engaged in the investigation, then will the activity have significant motivational value, and actually teach something!

I use films essentially for two purposes. First, if I have had students deep into an investigation that has involved a lot of tough primary sources, I often feel that their imaginations need a little help visualizing the real people and places we have been studying. I realize that there is a school of thought that condemns television for its numbing impact upon the imagination. However, I believe that in moderate doses films can actually assist the imagination. Young people have very limited experience, and imagination depends, to a great extent, upon one's experience in the world. If a child has never traveled, never looked carefully at a number of different landscapes, never met many people from diverse backgrounds, as is the case with most children, then it is hard for that child to do the visualizing and imagining that will make the people behind the words, strange syntax, and indecipherable scrawl of ancient sources come to life. A good film, especially a well-produced feature film, can help.

For example, when teaching about the social structure of early modern Europe, the setting for the forces behind European colonization of much of the world, I have students do a number of analytical and role-playing activities (one of which is discussed below), designed to reveal the great disparity in wealth, the impact of rapid population growth, and the importance of land ownership within the societies of western European countries. The film *The Return of Martin Guerre,* in spite of being a story about a little-known bunch of farmers in a remote region of France, provides an excellent illustration of the life that most Europeans led in the 1500s. The people that my students have seen in statistics and descriptive documents are portrayed in their dirt-covered clothes, laboring in their steaming fields, crowded in mud-swamped villages, strolling among the pigs and cattle, and celebrating pagan festivals that acquired Christian names during the Middle Ages. Thus, the willingness of yeomen and tenant farmers to travel three thousand miles across an angry ocean on the promise not of gold, but of free land, becomes more understandable with visualization. More important, there is that moment of "Ah, so · that's what it looked like," that adds a whole new dimension to the kids' discovery of the past. (Note of caution: *Martin Guerre* is "unrated," being a French film, but has a rather racey one-minute scene buried in the middle. Teenages love it, but their parents might not.)

My second purpose for using films is to raise the essential questions that will give direction to subsequent investigations. In fact, almost every time I show a film I preface the showing by asking students to jot down questions that come to their minds as they watch. Again, historical documentaries are unsuitable for this purpose, simply because their creators are deeply committed to providing answers! Feature films, on the other hand, very often beg some of the most important questions historians ask about the past. In *Martin Guerre,* for example, the heroine knowingly violates church and civil law, deceiving her family and village, in order to live with a man she loves, even though her husband, who left her, is still alive in parts unknown. Although she is roundly condemned for her actions once the truth is known, she is spared punishment on the grounds that "women are easily deceived." This plot line raises important questions about the status and expectations of women in early modern European society. Students often ask how European women were viewed in this way when so-called "less civilized" Native American women were considered more equal in their own societies. It does not take much, then, for me to encourage them to think about the kinds of interaction that would take place between two peoples who were so different from each other.

A number of years ago, PBS produced a three-hour dramatization of the English effort to establish a colony at Roanoak in the 1580s. My placement of this film early in my course "The World After Columbus," as described in Chapter 3, is another good example of the use of films for both visualization and stimulating curiosity. My students have just studied John White's journal, seeking clues to the mystery of what happened to "the Lost Colony." The film is well worth the three hours of class time, for it contains scenes that are perfect replicas of White's drawings of the Roanoaks and provides a good model of how historians create a story from old documents (the producers leave the mystery unsolved). Furthermore, it forces the questions of why Europeans were interested in colonization, how they ever managed to "succeed" at it, and why their encounters with the native peoples of the Americas resulted in bloodshed (for information on the film, see the appendix).

We are fortunate in New England to have a number of excellent historical sites, and for subjects such as colonialism, the evolution of democracy, industrialization, and the study of original peoples, many of these sites are excellent resources for world history courses. One of my favorite places is the Mashantucket Pequot Museum in Ledyard, Connecticut, where the Mashantuckets have spared no expense to tell their story. With colorful three-dimensional exhibits, dramatic films, computerized presentations, and a reconstructed village in which visitors wander among the wigwams listening to explanations of lifeways on digital speakerphones, the museum presents a tremendous quantity of information, all based on careful research. Students could spend several hours here and not be able to take in all that is offered about the history of the Pequots from the last ice age, through the arrival of the Europeans, and up to the present day. Furthermore, the technology is certainly designed to appeal to the digital generation.

Yet, with all that, the same cautions that apply to films must apply here. Students not focused on a particular investigation could easily become overwhelmed, or simply grow impatient, as children do, with all the information, and flit from one exhibit to the next, not giving anything enough time to become significant or interesting. I incorporate our visit into a two-week study of the Pequot War of 1637, which I will discuss below. We do not try to make use of the entire museum, but focus instead on those exhibits that provide information in our investigation into the causes and immediate outcomes of the war. The incorporation of this information into a larger quest, of which students feel some degree of ownership, results in a pleasant, exciting trip. What is even more thrilling for me are student comments about how much they would like to return to see the rest some day.

One certain advantage that historical sites have is that they are local! In saying that I am not thinking of the containment of travel costs, but the inherently motivating nature of "history in one's own backyard." Again, the power of the local element depends upon how the site visit is integrated into other investigations, but it is generally not too difficult to determine how history made close to home can fit into and illustrate the history of the world.

Doing so makes world history a lot more concrete, which is just what young people need. In Hartford, Connecticut, for example, a somewhat eccentric man named Sam Colt constructed what was probably the largest and best-equipped firearms factory of his time (1850s). The study of the Industrial Revolution would not be complete for me without at least a drive-by of the remains of this factory with its quirky, blue-star-studded, onion-shaped dome. There's something special about having one of the most innovative industrialists and salesmen in the world having set up shop just five minutes down the road from our school in Windsor. It was here that British industrialists began to notice that Americans were catching up. It was here that refugees from the 1848 revolutions in Europe found that they could live in peace, earn top dollar, and actually be courted by local politicians. It was from here that Colt shipped arms to both sides in the Crimean and the American Civil Wars, and here that the forty-five caliber "Peacemaker" revolver was manufactured—all great subjects for debate. I will have some more to say a little later on about the motivating power of local history when integrated into world history investigations. The point here is that it does not take much looking to find an "it happened right here" in any neighborhood.

Thus, films and trips are important for motivating students, but not necessarily by themselves. They become most helpful when they are combined with the discovery process that makes any form of history exciting. Students will not automatically retain, understand, or even care to understand the information films and trips provide simply because of the medium or the setting. However, a good movie or a well-developed historical site can help to stimulate curiosity, deepen imagination, provide interesting information, and inspire creativity when thoughtfully integrated into an exciting sequence of lessons.

Exploring, Experimenting, Discovering

There is probably no limit to the neat little gimmicks that a teacher could come up with to wake students up and get them to pay attention. I have seen teachers tell jokes, act weird, dress crazily, host trivia game shows, draw funny pictures on worksheets, give spell-binding lectures, choose teams for relay races (don't ask), create vast lists of topics for independent research (alias copying from randomly selected secondary sources), and award pizza for up to eight places in diorama contests (the contestants secretly being the students' parents, who, distressingly, don't get to eat the pizza). Without trying to condemn any of these techniques (or was it too obvious?), I'll just ask if their practitioners really think that more than 1 percent of their students will recall their time in history class as truly satisfying. (OK—so now I have to act like mine do. Well, here goes.)

Let's begin with the premise already suggested, that history in itself is exciting. And so, it follows that the most useful technique for making history *class* exciting would be to create historical exercises. Take, for example, the Pequot War of 1637. As mentioned in Chapter 3, study of this event can be helpful in gaining an understanding of encounters in North America in the early seventeenth century. My goal in this exercise, however, is not only to teach about what happened and why, but also to teach about what historians do, and why they like their work. The best way to explain to students about the nature of history is to have them do history.

I begin with a *short* piece that summarizes the beginnings of the New England colonies and provide a map of where these colonies were and what native peoples lived in the area. Then we move to a sheet of paper that offers contrasting perspectives on the outcome of the Pequot War, in which the Pequot people were all but wiped out: a quotation from a monument to John Mason, commander of the English forces (he "saved the settlements from destruction"); statements by Miantonomo (a Narragansett) and Tecumseh (a Shawnee of a later era) predicting a similar fate for their own people if they did not resist the "avarice and greed of the white man"; and finally a segment from William Bradford's *Of Plimoth Plantation*, in which Bradford attributes the smallpox epidemic that killed thousands of Indians and the burning alive of six hundred Pequots to a beneficent act of God. I ask students to come up with a list of questions, and to write down their initial impressions as to the cause and significance of the war. The quotations are so wide-ranging, and Bradford's description of the violence is so horrifying, that they cannot help but have ideas—and plenty of questions.

This is where I begin to tell them what historians do. The most important questions, I say, are the most difficult to answer—questions about why anyone would commit these acts, why people cannot get along better, why the violence continues to resonate in succeeding generations, and how anyone can tie religion to such horrors. These matters are precisely what historians try to understand. Yet, what makes the historian's trade most difficult is the fact that the people who were involved in all of this are dead and gone. We can't haul them all in and give them the third degree to get to the bottom of the matter. All we have left are a few scraps of paper, maybe some oral traditions passed down from generation to generation, the buried and fossilized remains of a village here, an old musket or sword there. And with that, we must come to some sort of understanding. The task is greatly complicated, of course, by all of the myth and legend making that has gone on since the event in question (which, sadly, includes what is written in many history textbooks).

So we look at some of the scraps of paper, the first in the collection I have prepared for them being excerpts from a narrative of the war written by

Captain John Mason. And what do we find? First of all, strange language and *s*'s that look like *f*'s (yes, I give them the real thing, not an edited and modernized version). Then, after considerable struggle trying to read what he wrote, we find that his story is not just the facts, but turns out to be a self-congratulatory, blame-shifting essay crammed with references to the glory of God as He inflicts severe punishment upon His enemies. How on earth can we wade through all of this biased material and discover the truth? Perhaps, some more scraps of paper will help.

Alas, there are no narratives written by the Pequots, but there are plenty of speeches that North American Indians have made regarding their often violent relationships with European immigrants. They may throw some light on the matter, as would some descriptions by eyewitnesses, anthropologists, and archaeologists of the way the indigenous people lived and viewed the world. We look at some of these speeches and descriptions and toss some ideas around about what they might mean. Then there are narratives of the war written by other Europeans, and some of them do not necessarily share Mason's view of the providential nature of the outcome. For example, poor Lion Gardiner, the Dutch engineer hired to build a fort at the mouth of the Connecticut River, warns that the English are the sinners, and had better rethink what they are doing before the tables turn on them and they end up skinned alive or impaled on a stake. By analyzing and comparing these accounts we can begin to peel away the layers of bias, separate fact from fabrication, and piece together a clearer picture of what was going on.

Another collection of documents offers contextual clues upon which historians rely for hints to the meaning that people attribute to other people's actions and for possible explanations for the actions they take in response. Included in these is the Treaty of Hartford (1643), which established a new division of power in New England, and letters by Roger Williams, John Winthrop, and other people from various places reporting on their contacts with Native American leaders and concerns those leaders had expressed to them. From this we begin to postulate on the motives behind Mohegan and Narragansett support for the English, the role that disease and the fur trade were playing in shaping kinship and political relationships among the various native peoples, and the dynamics of cultural change with all of these forces at work.

To be sure, I have not put together every known source that would bear on the questions we have asked about the Pequot War, and the seventeenth-century Pequots have very little chance to speak for themselves in the investigation. (Our subsequent trip to the Pequot Museum shows this, but at least casino revenues have allowed the twentieth-century Pequots the opportunity to offer a perspective.) Nevertheless, I think that my students have enough material by which they can develop some reasonable hypotheses about the causes of the war, or by which they can write a reasonably complete story. After they have done some serious writing, we talk about the problem of being confined by our own cultural and temporal limitations, realizing that even if all of the participants were here for us to interview—or even if we could somehow view the event through a time-telescope—we would be viewing with our own eyes—eyes that see what they are conditioned to see.

Is the elusiveness of objectivity too weird for adolescents to conceptualize? Do they just throw up their hands when the prospect of finding *the answer* becomes too complicated? If anything, I have found the opposite to be true. The deepest problems that historians face seem to be the major attractions of history for young people. Certainly it takes some discussion before they begin to move away from a conditioned need to arrive at a *the truth*. Students in prep schools in particular are very adept at searching out *the right answer*, but even they can be deconditioned to recognize how hard we have to work to get beyond our own cultural shells. Nevertheless, I have to say it is work they seem to thrive on.

In the appendix we note where to get the documentary materials for the Pequot War investigation. However, I should point out here that the excitement of this particular investigation is heightened for my students because the Pequot War is local history. Not only did it occur in Connecticut, but some of the main characters in the conflict actually lived in the meadow behind our school where my students play soccer and lacrosse. Now, this war does not usually rate more than a few sentences in most textbooks and is not mentioned in the World History Standards, but all the better! Students feel as though they are making a new discovery—uncovering hidden history. Here, along with the "backyard" dimension, is the other great advantage of local history: often the textbooks do not have much detail on it, and so students feel it can become "my history." They, not the text authors, are the owners. Thus, I am not suggesting that all teachers get the Pequot War documents and make that event a big part of their world history courses. It might be even better that they develop a set of documents on some local event so that their students can feel the joy of discovering the past for themselves.

Whatever the subject of exploration, no discovery is complete without its announcement—that is, a presentation to others of one's findings. In the case of the Pequot War, I have asked students to present their discoveries either in the form of a narrative of the war, or of an analytical essay on its causes. The element of authenticity enters in as they realize that real people of the present actually are concerned about what happened in the past, and why it happened. For the narrative assignment, students are completing the historian's work—they are writing the textbook themselves. Having brought the puzzle pieces together, using their own imagination, they must now engage the imaginations of an audience and tell a story that is close to the truth. Put that way, kids realize that writing history is a creative and artistic enterprise, as well as an exacting enterprise. It's not enough simply to list events in chronological order. They need to bring the past to life and let their audience share the experience, while at the same time being as true to the sources as possible. In effect, I have turned the tables: instead of my doing all of the work to explain what happened and to make the story exciting, it's their turn.

As for the analytical essay, I frame that in the form of a position paper for a public agency (the Connecticut Historical Commission) that is concerned about what to do with a statue of John Mason, the location of which (on the site of the fort he burned to the ground) was offensive to today's Pequots. This was actually a controversial issue here in Connecticut a few years ago. Furthermore, it continues to have local resonance, because the statue has been moved to Mason's hometown of Windsor, the town in which I teach. Every year since its transplanting, the statue has been subject to some form of protest or vandalism, even though its plaque no longer celebrates Mason's victory over the Pequots, but rather his extensive list of public offices. In entering into the fray over who or what is to blame for a 350-year-old war, students are entering the real world with all of its bitterness, continuing resentments (new ones too, such as bitterness over Indian exemption from gambling restrictions), and efforts at reconciliation.

Getting kids to write on this subject is not difficult at all. Whether they are skilled writers or still in the very-clumsy stage, I never fail to see leaps forward. And what is remarkable is that there is really no secret here, or if there is, it is simply that kids much prefer to be doing work that adults do, if they have to work at all, rather than some artificial collection of tasks that no one does outside of a classroom. Of course, there are other strategies, employed in the thinking phase, that contribute to the effort to make the writing of history exciting, and I will turn to these now. What I had hoped to offer first, though, is the premise that *doing* history, that is engaging in the exploration, experimenting, and discovering, is what will draw kids to the subject.

Free Thinking

Another name for experimenting, exploring, and discovering is "higher-order thinking." Actually there are a lot of names that have been used for the complex of cognitive activity that enables a historian to do his or her work well. And, in fact, most history teachers will tell you that thinking skills are a high priority for them. They want their students to be able to think analytically and imaginatively and to write and speak clearly and persuasively. The problem is not the perceived value of the thinking processes one can learn from a good history course. Rather, the problem is the same as it is with the subject matter itself: thinking always has the potential to become tedious. Besides framing historical thinking as an exercise in exploration of the real world, how do we get kids to stick with it and actually think *hard*?

There are a couple of principles by which I operate in addressing this challenge. First, it is important to work in manageable phases—that is, to avoid presenting the thinking side of the task as something that is only possible for someone who normally gets all A's and can easily make great abstract leaps. Second, kids need to be encouraged to *think freely* if we want them to get interested in thinking at all. And finally, as if it needs to be said (although it does), success is the best motivater.

The Roanoak exercise discussed in Chapter 3 is a good example of breaking up an historical inquiry into manageable phases and encouraging students of all abilities to move from the concrete to the abstract. It begins with an intriguing story of a desperate effort to get a colony "planted," and ends with John White's agonizing return to his "planters" three years later, only to find that they have disappeared. White's narrative of his attempts to find the people he left behind poses the problem, and immediately signals to students that what historians do first is to ask questions. What happened to the colony? Did they run out of supplies? Why could they not live off of the land? Were they attacked? Why couldn't they get along with the Native Americans? Did they go to live with the Croatoans with whom they did get along? Did that work out? Why did they get along with some of the natives but not with others?

At this point, as historians often do, we move to hypotheses—reasonable guesses as to what might have happened: they moved, they starved, they were killed, they became Croatoans, or they died trying to leave. Each of these is worth consideration against the evidence (that is, the clues that are left behind as we see them through John White's eyes). Of course, White may not see everything. He is not a trained detective (though he is a trained artist), and he did not have time to treat Roanoak Island as a crime scene. Nevertheless, historians do the best they can with what they have. We have not only his journal describing what happened before he left and what he found on his return (no houses, a palisade, pigs of iron, "CRO" carved on a tree, etc.), but we also have his drawings of the Roanoaks. Again, we are looking through his eyes, but it may be possible to use these to think about questions such as "Could the colonists survive without supplies?" After all, the Indians did. Or was it beyond the cultural capacity of English men and women to behave as "savages" and learn their survival skills?

I try to break down the process of historical inquiry into this episode into its traditional elements: questioning, hypothesizing, testing each hypothesis against the evidence, assessing the validity of the evidence chosen for analysis, and reconstructing the most likely course of events based upon that analysis. Along the way, there is ample time for each student to share in the process historians take on intuitively. The task becomes manageable, and they can see that they can indeed become historical thinkers. It helps in this case that historians have not been able to come up with *the answer*, and so no one needs to be frustrated about getting the wrong one.

As necessary as breaking up thinking tasks is for young historians, it is equally important to provide plenty of opportunities for wild, unbridled free thinking. The Pequot War unit discussed above provides a good illustration of a way to balance a structured approach to an inquiry with an element of creativity that can be enticing to young people. The technique here involves the use of freewriting. By that I mean asking students to keep a journal of their thoughts as they proceed through an inquiry, but also to assure them that for this portion of their work they need not think about organization, grammar, spelling, clarity, or even the quality of their big ideas. They should just write, and think, and write, and think—let it flow.

Figure 6–5 is a group of "reflections" from the journal of one of my tenth-grade students who was working on the Pequot War unit. Note that she is responding, first, to a steady barrage of new information, and second, to discussions that we are having in class as we go through the sequence of documents described above. What is important to see is that as she writes and writes, some very complex ideas work their way to the surface.

It might be noted that the development of an orderly hypothesis here has resulted from a disorderly approach. Thus, although it can be worthwhile to explain, model, and engage students in a step-by-step process of historical induction, as with the Roanoak exercise, it can be even more fun for students to be let loose to think freely. If they are encouraged to write as they think, then they can return to what they have thought and rethink, as historians often do—and rethink and rethink. In actuality, the inductive model provides a nice ideal and it makes theorizing seem manageable even to inexperienced thinkers; few historians reach conclusions as methodically as that. There is more experimentation, tentativeness, and spontaneous generation to it. And if we want students to experience what it is about history that we love, we need to encourage them to engage in the sort of wild thinking that makes history exciting. Instead of having their writing consist of a collection of careful notes, filled-out worksheets, and outlines, sometimes it is better to let them scribble randomly. The distinction is analogous to the difference between the neat and carefully organized lab notebooks that earn good grades in high school, and Einstein's notebooks, which you wouldn't believe if you saw them.

Embedded in the reflections in Figure 6–5 are references to work in a group. Without too much difficulty it should be possible to determine that the

A STUDENT WORKS HER WAY THROUGH THE SOURCES

Day 1 (after reading the background and differing perspectives)

I was surprised to find out that there was so much argument about the Pequot War. I can understand why the Indians would not look too favorably on it but when I read Bradford's description—he sounded like such a schmuck—all proud of himself for being English and the Pequots being burned to death like it was God's decision—and gloating about how the Naragansets were jumping around and celebrating. And why were they celebrating—in Mianotomo's speech he said the Pequots were right and because of the English "we shall all be starved." So why did he help the English fight the Pequots. I don't believe Bradford that the Pequots were warlike and hated by everyone, but I can't figure out any other reason why there own people would fight against them—didn't they all recognize how greedy the English were? Why didn't they all join up and wipe out the English? And how come John Mason is such a hero now? His statue in Windsor doesn't have the same plaque on it anymore, like he was some glorious savior—but he's all high and mighty bigger'n life drawing his sword right smack in the middle of the Windsor green like he's some god or something. This is all confusing—obviously we need to find out more about what happened in order to find out why it happened and who the real heroes were.

Day 2 (after reading about the Algonkians)

Before the whites came the Indians had a quiet and peaceful existence. but even before the settlers started to settle there were big problems—the indians felt cheated in trade, and were becoming dependent on the whites to give them metal and blankets in return for wampum that the whites used in the fur trade. Then the whites came and took something even more sacred—their land—the indians didn't understand property ownership. The land was their religion, and they couldn't sell it. No wonder they seemed savage to the whites. But all this still doesn't tell me why the Pequot war started, unless it was over the problem with the wampum—but even the naragansetss were annoyed about that, and they were on the English team.

Day 3 (after reading John Mason's narrative)

UN-BE-LIEV-ABLE. This guy is too much (once I deciphered all the *f*'s and *s*'s)—he thinks he's god's soldier saving the land from the heathen savages. What an unprincipled bloodthirsty animal—and my dorm is named after this clown. Why did he write all this—so we'd know what a barbarian he was??? I can't believe anything he says. He says the war all started because the Pequots killed Captain Stone—who knows—couldn't tell by believing this self-righteous slob. It was the Lord's doing It was the Lords doing!!! That's all he says. Oh, I'll just burn 300 pequots today—make god happy and stuff. And

Figure 6–5. *Pequot War student reflections*

who's this ONKOS guy who helps him? I still don't see why Miantonomo or Myantomo (can't they spell or what) helped the English, but I sure do see why the English attacked the pequots—they thought they were God's gift to the world and anyone who got in there way deserved to die. But were they really in the way of the English? I thought they'd been pretty much been cleaned out by smallpox like Bradford said—back in 1633. Or was that the other Indians on the Connecticut r.? I really need to read somebody else's version of this whole mess before I puke.

Day 4 (after reading other eyewitness accounts)

I'm beginning to see some things that are going on now. Especially Gardener gave me a lot of clues—this guy is really scared, and everything he reports is about how he's all boxed in in Saybrook and he didn't have the soldiers he was supposed to have, and his men got skinned alive and roasted and all that. Then he seems upset that the soldiers came and tried to teach the indians a lesson but what did he expect? I wonder if all these guys aren't just scared—they don't know the pequots, and all the indians in the area don't seem to think too much of the pequots—probably that's where Bradford got the idea that the pequots were warlike. But why didn't they just sit down and talk with each other??? I think I remember something about the Pequots going to Boston to try to talk things out—but the Mass bay people just asked them for wampum—bad idea. Then they get all huffy and demand the pequots fork up Stone and Oldhams killers—who says the pequots killed those guys anyway—and I think they're right—how were they supposed to tell Dutch from English, same old dirty and smelly Europeans as far as they were concerned. So then the English go on a killing rampage, and guess what!!! the Pequots start killing too. That was a no-brainer.

Day 5 (after reading the last set of documents)

so it goes in this order:

Uncas wanted to be Sachem of the pequots

Sassacus becomes sachem

June 1636 Uncas tells Brewster the Pequots are out to get him

August 1636 Roger Williams gets the Narragansetts not to join the peqots

1638 after the war—Uncas and the Nrgnts get slaves and land of the pequots

1643 Miantonomo gets axed for possibly conspiring against the English—by Uncas!

Hmmm. This uncas guy is a real slimeball. What does he get out of it? maybe there's something in the wampum thing. The English pigs were wrecking clam banks, and the piggy English wanted more and more wampum—who made the wampum and who got the shaft?

Figure 6–5. *Pequot War student reflections* (continued on page 156)

possible causes of the war:

> indians not united—fighting each other over the fur trade
> Pequots eliminated as middle-men when English go up river
> english think they are "Israel" and this is the promised land
> english greedy
> cultural differences—land owning, suspicion
> smallpox makes everybody cranky
> revenge killings
> misunderstandings: english/Dutch, who killed Stone, language issues
> smallpox not only makes people cranky, it makes indian leaders dead—
> > lots of fighting for power

(REGROUPED)

> Differences lead to conflict (cultural/religious, suspicions, resentments,
> > land issues, trade issues)
> English self-righteousness and greed
> Indian disunity
> Misunderstandings and revenge lead to escalating violence

Thesis our group will prove

The Pequot War was a big mess. Sure there were differences between the English and the Indians over religion, ways of life, who brought the plague, who owned the land and who ought to call the shots on trading. But all that could have been resolved if the English weren't so greedy. Another problem was that among the Indians there was a lot of conflict. Misunderstandings on all sides led to some unfortunate incidents which seemed to call for revenge, and from then on things just got worse. When it was all done, the Pequots didn't even have someone to tell their story for them.

Thesis our group will prove (rewritten)

The Pequot War was a complicated but not unavoidable tragedy. It's not surprising that two peoples as different as the American Indians and the English settlers, with their different outlooks, would not get along. After all, there was bound to be resentment as disease ravaged the Algonkians in the early 17th century and their ways of life shifted immensely because of new trading habits. There were other issues as well between the English and the Indians. However, the English could have been more understanding and open to negotiation. Furthermore, had it not been for conflicts among the Indians themselves, the English would probably have been forced to negotiate, and then all might have worked out their differences. Instead fear ruled the whole region and fed the fires of revenge, and when the English came out on top, they thought up excuses that made villains into heroes.

Figure 6–5. *Pequot War student reflections*

author of the reflections tended to be a leader within her small group—the rest of her group members did not have a journal that matched hers for insight. And yet, as a group, they functioned well, for the girl who wrote those reflections relied as much upon the others for their reaction and suggestions for revision as they relied upon her for leadership. In the end there was a sense that all had participated in the investigation in some way or another. That is, there was both group and individual ownership of the inquiry, and of the theories that came from that inquiry. The result was not only a fairly sophisticated theory, but also a general feeling of success on the part of everyone in the group. The result of that, in turn, was an observable increase in interest on the part of the "followers" in thinking about the complexities of events in subsequent investigations. In other words, success—that the students can claim as their own—is infectious.

That is why I try to offer as many modes of investigation as possible. If I encourage students to try their ideas out on each other, to write freely and let their ideas flow out randomly, or at other times to proceed in an orderly fashion in manageable steps, somewhere along the line every one of them is going to experience some measure of success. If we are not too insistent upon everyone being good at every type of activity, they might just get excited enough by their accomplishments in one area to begin to excel in another. By the way, I am not avoiding in-depth discussion of the psychological basis of this notion, as well as others, in this chapter because I do not think that attention to child psychology is important in understanding motivation. I am just hoping to emphasize the inherently motivating nature of historical inquiry itself. We should be aware of what makes young people tick, but we do not have to go beyond the discipline for the stimuli that makes them tick better.

Play

Success is one good teacher, probably the best, but in all that has been said so far, it should be possible to observe that "play" is also an important teacher. The reason is that play embodies some of the attributes of success—or, to put it another way, success is more likely in a playful situation.

Students love acting, and when encouraged to ham it up, they actually can demonstrate some very sophisticated understanding of the material under study. Trials can be a lot of fun, especially when they personify difficult issues. For example, Elizabeth I of England was faced with the serious challenge of formulating a policy on religion that would work for a nation torn by dissent and political intrigue. The terms of the Anglican Settlement are a matter of record, but what exactly did it mean to "walk the middle road" between Catholicism and the more radical forms of Protestantism, while allowing some measure of toleration? In 1581 she had to deal with a Jesuit priest,

Edmund Campion, who professed loyalty to her, but insisted on traveling about England in an effort to convert people to the Catholic Church. A classroom trial of Campion, with Elizabeth, Campion, members of Parliament, and nobles of various religious persuasions can get a little anachronistic, but it can also be a captivating way of gaining a sophisticated understanding of the complexities of the queen's policies in an increasingly dangerous world.

Negotiating sessions are also quite worthwhile, for they help students realize how difficult some decisions are. In both world history courses at Loomis Chaffee we reenact a conference that took place in the kingdom of Dahomey on the West African coast in 1715. Present at the conference were numerous slave traders from European nations, King Agaja of Dahomey and a number of his supporters, and quite a few local people who had concerns about the impact of the slave trade on their lives and who hoped that the king would take these into acount.[1] Agaja was facing a dilemma. He relied upon the slave trade for the weapons and other resources that kept him in power, and yet, he faced considerable internal dissension because of the constant state of warfare his subjects endured. The stability of his kingdom, in other words, was dependent upon the instability of his region.

During the role play, the various characters negotiate with Agaja through moderators, trying to make him understand their diverse needs and goals, and then Agaja announces his decision. The students then read about the actual outcome (eventual disintegration of Dahomey), and discuss the relationship between internal politics in West Africa and the expansion of the Atlantic slave trade. A consideration of the horrors of the "middle passage" is also part of the follow-up lesson. While the realizations that students come to could not be characterized as "fun," the experience of acting out varying perspectives in an actual event is accompanied by a good deal of excitement.

Occasionally I will take on a role, myself, in these activities, in order to stir up some additional excitement and controversy, or just to serve as a somewhat crazy model of how interesting the activity can become when the role players work hard to portray the subtleties of the role and make relationships to elements of the context in which the reenacted event occurs. My colleague Bob Andrian is also famous for his costumed appearances as various historical characters, particularly his appearance at the Alhambra banquet. This is a major event for world history students at Loomis Chaffee, combining the motivating power of socializing, food, colorful costumes, and role playing, all tried-and-true strategies for adolescents.

Role playing in writing can also be both enlightening and fun. I have had students imagine and create diary entries, letters, editorials, pamphlets, legislative bills, and many other types of documents that would have been written at the time under study. The following is a writing assignment I have given at the conclusion of a unit of study on the changes that have taken place in the

British colonial society along the eastern North American seacoast in the early 1700s (as discussed in Chapter 3). I have always been pleased with the depth and sophistication of the results I get from students on this assessment, and I attribute most of that success to the enthusiasm with which they approach being a spy (and with which they approach the idea of having food afterward! Ah—the three shining stars of adolescent motivation: success, play, and food).

April 27, 1752

Most Secret Memorandum to: M. Michel Guillaume Jean de Crèvecoeur
From: His Excellency the Governor of New France, the Marquis Duquesne
Subject: Our Neighbors to the South

M. Crèvecoeur:

You have served ably over the past four months as our aide-de-camp, and we have valued most highly all of your activity on our behalf, as well as, and in particular, your advice on most pressing matters of policy. It is our opinion that you are blessed with a particular gift of insight into the souls of humankind, and that we may depend upon you to give us a frank estimate of what lies in their minds and how we may expect they will respond in various instances, etc. etc. etc.

Be all that as it may, it is our purpose to discover as much as possible about our neighbors to the South. As you well know, the British government has for these 150 years been most active and engaged in planting settlers in that region below the St. Lawrence and above the Floridas, and are even now threatening our interests below the Lakes and in the Ohio Valley. In the last conflict (1744–1748) they became most annoying and we were inconvenienced in many ways. The English forces of combined regular troops and colonial irregulars captured our fort at Louisbourg, and it was only with the most artful negotiations (not to mention the offering of a few choice Caribbean islands) that the post was returned to us at the end of the war. Now we must prepare ourselves in the event that another conflict erupts, and we must know all we can about this rabble.

We say rabble, for we know not how else to characterize the society they have constructed in those parts. Our sources say they have not only the English settlers and the Indians living there, as we have French and Indians living here, but also have great numbers of Africans among them, mostly enslaved, although some are free. These sources also say that whereas we have but one faith (aside from the lingering superstitions of our Indians who are not yet converted to the true faith), they have a number of faiths and are much distracted, in fact, by recent calamities resulting therefrom. Further, they say there are not only English settlers, but their white settlers include persons from a great many other Europeans countries, many of whom do not speak English. And whatever their origin, each small region has developed its own customs and seems most dissimilar to that of the mother country! Finally, we have learned that there are even hostilities within each region. All this, as you can imagine, is a great delight to hear of, for with such disunity it seems we could make quick work of conquering the lot of them. Still, it seems a shame to consider doing such to what appears to be a most interesting society.

Therefore, YOUR ORDERS:

1. You will proceed to the junction of the Allegheny and the Monongahela Rivers where we are constructing a new fort to protect the eastern frontier of our fur trading territory. There you will receive guidance from Colonel LaPeletier as to the best way to infiltrate the British domain at the city of Philadelphia, some 300 miles east. This will be an arduous journey, so prepare for the worst.

2. Once you have entered the British domain you will visit their colonies in the South, in the middle zone, and in the North and observe and record all you see. We leave the particulars to you, for you always seem to know what is worth understanding about people—but do keep in mind that we truly wish to *understand* this rabble, as we call it, at its deepest level. Our only suggestion is that you interview various persons of all classes and situations in order to incorporate as many perspectives as possible into your understanding.

3. You will send your report to us by Monday, the 15th instant. As always it will be marked by the following characteristics:

An introduction which acknowledges receipt of these instructions, *clearly* demonstrates your understanding of the purpose of this investigation, and provides a *clear and succinct* overview of the society you have observed.

A particular discussion of each of the elements of the overview—said discussion to be *fact-filled*, relating examples from your various interviews and observations.

Within the discussion you should also make note of important *changes* which have occurred in that part of America over the past fifty years, in all the *complexity* you perceive.

A summary, which not only reviews the overview, but also provides us with your frank opinion as to whether or not we will need to invade at all (that is, perhaps the society will simply disintegrate under its own internal tensions, or become so far different from their mother country as to separate and set up for themselves—and then will be much weakened by the lack of military help from Britain).

4. In general, Michel, what makes these Americans tick, if we may use the metaphor of the clock so often referenced by our esteemed philosophes? Good luck, and God Bless. Send your report through channels when you reach Boston. We will see to your extraction should your office and mission be discovered. On your return we shall have banquet.

Duquesne

One final type of role-playing activity that is exciting and energizing is the simulation game. In "The World After Columbus" we fight the battle of the Spanish Armada (a board game), negotiate the various trump cards that Charles I and the English Parliament had in their hands (a card game), and sail the Atlantic hoping to amass a fortune in the world trading system of the early 1700s (a board game/computer simulation/negotiation tumult).[2] My colleague David Beare and I created a simulation game of our own in order to teach the economic and social impact of the rapid population growth in western Europe in the late sixteenth and early seventeenth centuries. In "People, Prices and Products" each student assumes the role of a person living in a local economy: Gentleman, Tenant Farmer, Artisan, Landless Laborer, and so on. The players have to negotiate rent, sales of goods (at gyrating prices), marriages, distribution of land, and wage contracts, as well as make decisions on their own about which fields to plant with what crops, whether to abandon farming altogether and learn a trade, whether to raise a family, and a number of other issues. As the game progresses from session to session, they experience the vagueries of weather, the ups and downs of the business cycle, and the overall decline in wages and rise in agricultural prices that was characteristic of the era. To be sure, the experience requires a good deal of processing once the game is over, at which time students can stand back from the fray and think about what was happening to the economy as a whole. Nevertheless, I have found that the fun of the game itself raises the interest level in what for most can be a rather dry investigation into socioeconomic processes (see the appendix for information on obtaining this game).

Finally, returning to the notion with which I began this chapter, it is possible to turn document analysis itself into a playful enterprise. This is particularly the case with materials that lend themselves to quantitative analysis, such as records of individual communities. There have been a number of studies of the Salem witch scare of 1692, for example, that can serve as models for the use of tax, vital, and land records in historical inquiry.[3] Students may be able to find similar types of materials on their own communities, as did the Hartford "Cities" students described in Chapter 2. Or there are often printed records of particular communities in both Europe and the Americas. One such collection, "The Records of Earles Colne, 1350–1850," an English parish in Essex, can even be found on the Internet. With tax, land, birth, death, and marriage records students can create charts and graphs to explore all sorts of dimensions of human experience in this small village. The data also lends itself well to the use of a computer database program, which can be fun once students learn to manipulate data electronically. It is remarkable how enthusiastically students take to fussing around at tasks even many historians consider tedious.

In this chapter I have tried to offer not so much a how-to manual regarding motivation, but rather an argument. That is, I have proposed that history is exciting all by itself. There is no need for gimmicks to "spice it up," for what could be more exciting than the vast spectrum of human experience itself. Clearly, teachers want to be selective about the events, topics, and issues they work on with their students, not only in terms of what is appropriate, but also in terms of what will be intriguing to students of various backgrounds, ages, localities, and abilities. It is the exploration itself, however, that engages them, and there is, as we all will insist, no greater exploration than that which travels into the past for understanding. As Lou Ratté wrote in Chapter 4, teachers who engage in critical reading, research, and investigation of new subjects themselves are well aware of what history really is all about, and make better teachers as a result. The same can be said for our students. How can we deny them that which has made us lovers of history?

Notes

1. This role play was actually created by a student of mine, Carey Franklin, who did the research on the event, put together a collection of primary and secondary source reading materials, some of which she wrote herself, and developed role-play information sheets on twelve individuals. The appendix explains how to acquire this material.

2. All of these originated from EDC with their course "From Subject to Citizen," although I have added considerably to the complexities of "The Game of Empire," with additional interest groups and using a Filemaker Pro database to keep track of the flow of goods in a surreal manner that makes my classroom seem like a commodities exchange pit.

3. Paul Boyer and Stephen Nissenbaum, *Salem Possessed: The Social Origins of Witchcraft* (Cambridge: Harvard University Press, 1974); Carol Karlsen, *The Devil in the Shape of a Woman: Witchcraft in Colonial New England* (New York: Norton, 1987); Enders Robinson, *The Devil Discovered: Salem Witchcraft 1692* (New York: Hippocrence Books, 1991).

Epilogue

W hat do we mean to convey when we call ourselves and our book an exploration of world history? In what sense do we consider ourselves explorers, and what do we mean when we state as an objective that students consider themselves as explorers? In the most obvious sense, we acknowledge that world history as currently taught and discussed is a new subject. We each have our different ways of emphasizing that point. Bob Andrian distinguishes world history today from its nineteenth- and early twentieth-century forebears; Mark Williams sees its current origins in the intellectual upheavals of the 1960s; and Lou Ratté sees its most interesting scholarship in the critical movements of the late 1970s, 1980s, and 1990s. We are explorers in that we think world history today is open territory: what to teach under that rubric and how to teach it are issues that are currently open-ended. We hope our essays will help other teachers take advantage of the opportunities for intellectual growth that that open-endedness makes possible.

Pedagogical Issues

Our concerns with what to teach are inextricably linked to how to teach, and hence each of us pays a lot of attention to pedagogical issues. Our similarities here are at least partially explained by our having worked together as history teachers for nine years; and our differences have to do with who we are, how we came to our interest in world history, and where our academic interests are rooted.

On the question of our similarities, we can each credit one another with our shared belief in the importance of engaging students in the study of history through practices that spark the imagination at the same time that they stimulate the intellect. Hence our enthusiasm for role play, reenactments, and other kinds of participatory activities. In the second part of the book we give our sense of what student engagement can mean. Of the three of us, Mark has chosen to deal most directly with motivation. He shares with Bob a desire to have students *do* history, and he has gone to greater length than Bob and Lou to help us understand what he means by that. Students watch full-length feature films (not documentaries) in order to be able to visualize the past, since they lack the experience of adults; they go on field trips to museums and historic sites, armed with research agendas, engage in role plays, and undertake projects in local history. They play games, are encouraged to think freely about subjects they are investigating, and take on the persona of people in the past. Mark sees these activities as enabling students to experience some sense of ownership of their own historical inquiry.

Though, of course, the subjects his students investigate are highly structured by him, Mark considers that through their activities students are actually doing history, or at least sharing some of the joys that historians experience when they do history. We can understand this point if we consider the breadth of Mark's definition of history. He sees history as the search, the document, the process, the thing we love. At one place he defines history as a combination of analysis and imagination. At other places he has recourse to metaphor: history is what lies beneath the layers of obscurity, a puzzle, and he, the historian, is at the controls of a time machine. History in the general sense, rather than world history in particular, is a certain style of questioning, the ability to put questions into a framework that incorporates agreed-upon ingredients: forces, events, context, outcomes. History is certainly still about change, but change as a guiding concept has expanded under Mark's microscope to require consideration of multiple perspectives, distant and current trends, events, people. In Mark's view, historical inquiry has to grasp the complexity that people themselves grasped, and the added complexity that time and distance from the events in question have enabled us to see. History is the study of the past in all its complexity, shorn of the value-laden devices that enabled us to select a single stream in the flow of time as more significant than the whole. This is a big order, and it is no wonder that Mark's goal is to create lifelong learners.

Bob also wants his students to be lifelong learners, but he puts more emphasis on having students emerge from the study of world history as world citizens, aware a little more than they were before the course, of where they come from as individuals and especially as members of groups and nations. What are their responsibilities as citizens of the world? Surely, one such responsibility is to dispel ignorance wherever it surfaces to deflect attention away from our shared humanity. The centerpiece of Bob's course is a banquet, held in Spain in 1492, bringing together (with considerable artistic license) the famous and not so famous from around the world: luminaries of the Islamic world, leaders of the scholastic world of European Christianity, and inventors from Asia, for a grand celebration of world harmony. This magnificent banquet is rudely interrupted by the arrival of the Grand Inquisitor and the monarchs Isabella and Ferdinand, ready to drive the last of the Muslims out of Spain, end the Reconquest, and (as we know) send Spain forward into world conquest. The problem for students is to understand what shattered that harmonious vision.

As Lou reflects in Chapter 4, it becomes clearer that in her exploration of how to create a curriculum that was non-Eurocentric, she gave a good deal of attention to postcolonial scholarship, that body of work that has mushroomed since the late 1970s and the publication of Edward Said's *Orientalism*. In this body of scholarship she sees the potential for moving beyond the range of the European voice in order to hear the voices of those caught up in the process of European expansion, but at the receiving end. In her work during and after her involvement in the project she describes in Chapter 2, she has explored the possibilities for making use of this scholarship in the world history survey. Though more understated than Bob or Mark, Lou believes that scholarship that reveals a new perspective on what we thought we knew is itself motivating; for teachers, at least, learning is its own reward.

World History as a Teaching Subject

As explorers, we hope we have whetted your appetite for the voyages that you might take, on your own and with your students, as Mark does; with your department colleagues and the many groups offering assistance to world history teachers, as Bob does; and as a scholar consultant collaborating with teachers and students, as Lou does.

One of the most important ports of call on that voyage is the consideration of what world history is. Since none of us consider world history to exist as a thing out there, we will leave aside the issue of the relationship between the past and what historians write about it to address a more manageable question. Is world history a teaching subject or a research subject?

We three agree that world history, whatever else it may be, is emphatically a teaching subject with a mission to perform. Whether that mission be understood as creating lifelong learners, world citizens, or patient trackers of contemporary scholarship, the common goal is to help students better understand the world that they share with all other human beings. Though easy enough to say, the mission that we attribute to the world history course is not easy to achieve, and as we think we have demonstrated, the three of us are dissatisfied with the idea of world history as only a teaching subject, to be organized in the most expeditious way by linking together generalizations that have been made by others who, themselves, are examining the work of still others who have done the monographic research. In other words, we do not find the synthetic textbook approach useful.

It is not just that we are ornery. When we each began the work of designing our world history courses, as short a period of time as ten years ago, satisfactory models did not exist, or at least we did not find any. All three of us discovered early on that studying world history involved unlearning things that we had taken for granted. Just what is it that we think young people and adults (including ourselves) have to unlearn? What is it that we want to shock our audiences out of?

This knotty question is easiest for Mark to address because he is working primarily with areas (the Atlantic world) with which most of us feel culturally familiar. Mark recognizes multiple perspectives primarily within the early modern American and European worlds he investigates, even though he calls our attention to voices at the other side of encounters and wants students to explore on their own areas of the world not directly covered in his course outline. The question of multiple perspectives is most vividly demonstrated in the example Mark gives of the documents from Simsbury concerning grants of dangerous lands to marginal types as part of elite colonial policy. The story of those marginal types was lost to the historical record of colonial land tenure, and in calling it to our attention Mark makes use of the techniques and strategies of social history to reveal class distinctions. Without such documents, and the historian with the skills to interpret them, we would all be content with the story of colonial land policy as told by elites who situate themselves as representatives of the whole of their society. Mark's technique with us, as well as with his students, is to show through the modeling of historical inquiry, how what might appear to be utterly arbitrary and local can, in fact, take us to the heart of power relations in a particular society.

Bob makes more direct use of recent world historical literature in which issues of perspective are directly raised. He uses critical analyses of geographic practice to design an introductory lesson aimed at encouraging students to articulate what they think maps are. Once they have done so, Bob leads them through an exercise designed to help them discover on what grounds we can say that a map represents the perspective of the mapmaker and is not an unmediated representation of reality. While Mark encourages us to realize that historical inquiry can shake us out of the complacency that came about through listening only to the voices of the dominant, Bob asks us to avail ourselves of current critical literature in order to arm ourselves with insights that we might never have on our own.

Lou uses visual images and recent scholarship on museums and museum practice to help students and teachers discover the assumptions they have, as Americans, about the cultural authenticity of art works from outside Europe and the United States. She then suggests how new scholarship on the study of objects can provide ways of seeing how the world becomes culturally interconnected at the very time (late nineteenth century) when European and American anthropologists are emphasizing cultural difference.

As a teaching subject, which we certainly acknowledge world history to be, not only in our classrooms, but in the many manuals, how-tos, textbooks, document collections, teacher workshops, and conferences, world history demands an organizing principle. We wish to emphasize here that our experiences have taught us two things about the problem of the organizing principle, or conceptualization: (1) as course designers, whether we are teachers, scholarly consultants, or curriculum specialists, we have to take responsibility for choosing the organizing principle; and (2) the conceptual scheme that we choose is not arbitrary but must be clearly situated within a recognizable body of scholarship, whether that be social history, cultural history and postcolonial studies, the emerging discipline of world history, or some combination of these and other specializations. And although we admit that there can be better and worse choices, we do not accept the view that there is a correct choice.

Each of us has relied on professional colleagues, institutions, and publications in order to make our own conceptualizations of the world history course. What we feel to be essential, and what we encourage our readers to undertake, is the exploration of what, from the vast wealth of thought about the past, they consider to be workable for them, something they can affirm and for which they can take responsibility. For all of us, without exception, I think, this exploration must be a collegial and collaborative one. Our collective understanding of the past is changing rapidly as more and more work is being done by scholars to synthesize the work of their colleagues. Teachers need to work collaboratively with scholars in order to keep abreast of changing understanding. And scholars need to work with teachers if they want their work to be more generally understood.

In a way, we are touching here upon the issue of coverage, but it is also more than that. The coverage question as it has been raised usually presupposes that we could lay out all the events of the past with their causes and consequences, and decide which to emphasize and which to subordinate. What we are suggesting here is that there is an underlying question we need to ask about all those events: if we try to broaden our vision to include events and people previously relegated to insignificance, what new patterns can we see for organizing our understandings of the past? For instance, if we credit Lou's anonymous African art traders and Japanese cultural entrepreneurs with a role in shaping the international art market, how does our general understanding of international markets change? If we follow Bob's advice and accept Michel-Rolph Trouillot's view of the French during the Haitian Revolution as incapable of understanding the Haitian bid for freedom, what methods should we then use to try and recapture the motivation of the Haitians and other nonliterate revolutionary groups around the world?

Should world history be exclusively about the little guy (or the little gal)? Our answer is NO, emphatically, but the existing body of historical scholarship calls seriously into question any historical approach that continues to exclude ordinary people. We have to teach students how to ask the questions that historians are asking, Mark emphasizes; and, as Lou would respond, that means we have to help students and teachers grasp the interdisciplinary nature of historical inquiry today. We have to make sure that students are aware of *all* the different kinds of questions historians are now asking.

World History as a Research Subject

As history teachers, we all find ourselves having engaged in an undertaking that, to some extent, we fell into and then embraced. In that sense, we feel affinity with our students and are able to cast ourselves as explorers. As teachers, we of course rely on those aids and resources which are available for those who are primarily interested in world history as a teaching subject. The research side of world history interests us as well, and each for slightly different reasons. Mark is committed to social history and the study of everyday life, and that has taken him into the specialized literature on that subject, and thus into an interdisciplinary inquiry that will encompass insights from philosophy, political science, anthropology, literary theory, and history. His interest in encounter is also directing him to anthropological literature on areas outside the West where encounters took place, and thus to the critiques of anthropology of the 1980s and after. We have all discovered that when the world is the context, the multidisciplinary approaches that together have yielded up our object of study are becoming tightly interwoven.

Bob is hoping to enlist his department colleagues once again in order to work up a two-year American and world history combination. If the new course is also to be constructed around the concept of cultural encounter, Bob has rich materials to draw on in the American context. Not only is there a wealth of material on the American Indian and European encounter, but there is also a new interest in seeing how encounter materials on the Americas fit with materials on English and British encounters with peoples who became colonial subjects. Equally important is the extensive archive of African American and Afro-Caribbean experience that can be drawn on for the world history survey.

Lou wants to effect a synthesis between critical postcolonial scholarship and world history so that the concerns of postcolonials are not lost as the subject of world history develops. She shares with Mark the belief that the seemingly insignificant people of the world must find their place in history, but doubts that social history inquiry alone will be able to recover them for historical study. She shares with Bob the belief that encounter literature attempts to give us both sides of the story of the world's peoples meeting each other, and is convinced that in postcolonial scholarship we have the best means to explore that story from the perspective of the less powerful.

Each of us is aware that three things have happened in world history since 1990: (1) the teaching of world history has become institutionalized, in journals, workshops, conferences, websites, the National Standards, and the new Advanced Placement test; (2) research scholars with specializations in specific world areas have moved into the new field of world history, bringing their specialized interests with them, but with the intention of working comparatively and exploring the possibilities for an integrated world history; and (3) graduate degrees in world history are now being offered in history departments around the country. These three developments make regarding world history as both a teaching and a research subject an imperative for all teachers of the subject.

The Call to Action

How do we think our book can serve the needs of world history teachers? We are aware that teachability will always be uppermost in teachers' minds as they set about to organize materials for students. How many times have we all lamented that a particular source or idea is just great but would never work with students? It is over the issue of teachability that many of us, all of us some of the time, have succumbed to the allurements of the textbook. We do not want to dismiss textbooks out of hand, but we do want to encourage teachers to explore different ways of approaching the teachability issue.

All three of us, in developing our world history courses, have written some of our own materials. We have been aware that the ways in which we have conceptualized the course, and worked our ways through what we want students to learn, seem to demand primary or secondary sources that we have been unable to find. This awareness demonstrates most dramatically for us, and we hope for our readers, just how open-ended the subject of world history is, and how little of what falls under that rubric is easily available for teaching at all levels. Indeed, there is as yet no consensus on what students at different levels of schooling should learn in a world history course, just as there is no consensus on what a student graduating from high school or finishing the first two years of college should have learned in world history. The very fact that the subject is open-ended is what makes our interest in it so compelling and challenging. We have all discovered that for this subject, as Bob and Mark emphasize, we have to *do* history, which is to say that we actually have to ourselves write some of the materials that students will use. Here we would like to emphasize that doing history in this sense means making connections, building bridges, synthesizing, which in Mark's terms could be called the final conclusion to historical inquiry: presentation to an audience. We haven't found any way around this obligation in organizing our courses, and hence we recommend it as a responsibility that teachers of world history must be ready to take on. We all have to contribute to the making of this subject, since we are privileged to be teaching it before the bones of consensus have had time to stiffen.

Appendix
Resources for Teaching World History

Primary Source Books and Readers

Andrea, A., and J. Overfield, eds. 2001. *The Human Record: Sources of Global History.* 4th ed. 2 vols. Boston: Houghton Mifflin.

Clark, L. 1988. *Through African Eyes.* 2 vols. New York: Center for International Training and Education.

Ebrey, P. 1993. *Chinese Civilization: A Sourcebook.* 3d ed. New York: Free Press.

Hughes, S., and B. Hughes, eds. 1997. *Women in World History.* 2 vols. Armonk, NY: M. E. Sharpe.

Johnson, D., J. Johnson, and L. Clark. 1999. *Through Indian Eyes: The Living Tradition.* New York: Apex Press.

Kishlansky, M., ed. 1998. *Sources of World History: Readings in World Civilizations.* 2 vols. New York: Wadsworth.

Lu, D. 1997. *Japan: A Documentary History.* Armonk, NY: M. E. Sharpe.

Lunenfeld, M. 1991. *1492: Discovery, Invasion, Encounter. Sources and Interpretations.* Lexington, MA: D. C. Heath.

Moss, W., J. Terry, and J.-H. Upshur, eds. 1999. *The Twentieth Century: Readings in Global History.* Boston: McGraw-Hill.

Pearson, R., and L. Clark. 1993.*Through Middle Eastern Eyes.* New York: Center for International Training and Education.

Reilly, K., ed. 1995. *Readings in World Civilizations.* 2 vols. New York: St. Martin's.

———, ed. 2000. *Worlds of History: A Comparative Reader.* 2 vols. Boston: Bedford/St. Martin's.

Roupp, H., and D. Maier. 1991. *Treasures of the World: Literature and Source Readings for World History.* Atlanta: Scott, Foresman.

Schwartz, S., L. Wimmer, and R. Wolff, eds. 1998. *The Global Experience: Readings in World History.* 2 vols. New York: Longman.

Sherman, D., ed. 1995. *Western Civilization: Sources, Images, and Interpretations.* 4th ed. 2 vols. New York: McGraw-Hill.

Sherman, D., A. T. Grunfeld, G. Markowitz, D. Rosner, and L. Heywood. 1998. *World Civilizations: Sources, Images, and Interpretations.* 2 vols. Boston: McGraw-Hill.

Stearns, P., ed. 1998. *World History in Documents: A Comparative Reader.* New York: NYU Press.

Wiesner, M., W. B. Wheeler, F. Doeringer, and M. Page. 2001. *Discovering the Global Past: A Look at the Evidence.* 2d ed. 2 vols. Boston: Houghton Mifflin. A particularly useful and innovative source. See also the authors' *Discovering the Western Past* and *Discovering the American Past,* two-volume sets from Houghton Mifflin.

Selected Secondary Sources: General Reading in World History and Teaching Guides

Adas, M. ed. 1993. *Islamic and European Expansion: The Forging of a Global Order.* Critical Perspectives on the Past. Philadelphia: Temple University Press.

Bentley, Jerry H. 1998. "Hemispheric Integration, 500–1500 C.E." *Journal of World History* 9: 237–54.

———. 1993. *Old World Encounters: Cross-Cultural Contacts and Exchanges in Pre-Modern Times.* New York: Oxford University Press.

———. 1996. *Shapes of World History in Twentieth-Century Scholarship.* Washington, DC: American Historical Association.

Blaut, J. 1993. *The Colonizer's Model of the World: Geographical Diffusion and Eurocentric History.* New York: Guilford Press.

Boorstin, D. 1983. *The Discoverers.* New York: Random House.

Crosby, A. 1993. *Ecological Imperialism: The Biological Expansion of Europe, 900–1900.* Studies in Environment and History. Reissue. Cambridge: Cambridge University Press.

———. 1972. *The Columbian Exchange: Biological and Cultural Consequences of 1492.* New ed. Westport, CT: Greenwood.

Curtin, P. 2000. *The World and the West: The European Challenge and the Overseas Response in the Age of Empire.* Cambridge: Cambridge University Press.

Diamond, J. 1997. *Guns, Germs and Steel: The Fates of Human Societies.* New York: W. W. Norton.

Dunn, R., ed. 2000. *The New World History: A Teacher's Companion.* Boston: Bedford/St. Martin's.

Dunn, R., and D. Vigilante, eds. 1996. *Bring History Alive! A Sourcebook for Teaching World History.* Los Angeles: National Council for the Social Studies.

Encyclopedia of World Art. 17 vols. London: McGraw-Hill, 1967. The website for the Firenze fresco *Enthronement of St. Thomas* is: <www.kfki.hu /~arthp/html/a/andrea/firenze/index.html>.

Flynn, D. O., and A. Giraldez. 1995. "Born with a 'Silver Spoon': The Origin of World Trade in 1571." *Journal of World History* 6: 2201–21.

Frank, A. 1998. *ReORIENT: Global Economy in the Asian Age.* Berkeley: University of California Press.

Hodgson, M. 1993. *Rethinking World History: Essays on Europe, Islam, and World History.* Edited by Edmund Burke III. Studies in Comparative World History. Cambridge: Cambridge University Press.

Johnson, J., and D. Johnson. 2000. *The Human Drama.* Princeton, NJ: Markus Wiener.

Lewis, M., and K. Wigen. 1997. *The Myth of Continents: A Critique of Metageography.* Berkeley: University of California Press.

Linebaugh, P., and M. Rediker. 2000. *The Many-Headed Hydra: Sailors, Slaves, Commoners, and the Hidden History of the Revolutionary Atlantic.* Boston: Beacon Press.

Mitchell, J., H. B. Mitchell, W. Klingaman, and R. K. McCaslin, eds. 1998. *Taking Sides: Clashing Views on Controversial Issues in World Civilizations.* 2 vols. Guilford, CT: Dushkin.

Monmonier, M. 1995. *Drawing the Line: Tales of Maps and Cartocontroversy.* New York: Henry Holt.

National Center for History in the Schools. 1996. *National Standards for World History.* Los Angeles: National Center for History in the Schools.

Pomeranz, K., and S. Topik. *The World That Trade Created: Society, Culture, and the World Economy, 1400–The Present.* Sources and Studies in World History. Armonk, NY: M. E. Sharpe.

Reilly, K. 1989. *The West and the World: A History of Civilization.* New York: Harper & Row.

Reilly, K., and L. Shaffer. 1995. *The American Historical Association's Guide to Historical Literature.* 3d ed. Vol. 1. Edited by Mary Beth Norton. New York: Oxford University Press. A comprehensive, annotated list of works in the field of world history.

Roupp, H., ed. 1997. *Teaching World History: A Resource Book.* Sources and Studies in World History. Armonk, NY: M. E. Sharpe.

Trinkle, D., and S. Merriman, eds. 2000. *The History Highway 2000: A Guide to Internet Resources.* Armonk, NY: M. E. Sharpe.

Videos and CD-ROMs

Black Robe. 1992. Directed by Bruce Beresford. 128 min. Vidmark, Inc. Samuel Goldman Entertainment. Videocassette (Feature film).

Black Sugar: Slavery from an African Perspective. 1993. 28 min. Films for the Humanities, Inc. Videocassette.

The Columbian Exchange. 1991. Produced for PBS by WGBH, et al. 58 min. Films for the Humanities, Inc. Seven videocassettes.

Gandhi. 1982. Directed by Richard Attenborough. 160 min. Columbia Tri-Star Video. Videocassette.

Journeys Along the Silk Road. 2000. Produced by the Asia Society. New York, NY. CD-ROM.

The Name of the Rose. 1986. Directed by Jean-Jacques Arnaud. 128 min. Videocassette.

Roanoak. 1990. Produced by the Public Broadcasting System. 180 min. Video-cassettes.

Sankofa. 1995. Directed by Haile Gerima. 130 min. Mypheduh Films, Inc. Washington, D.C. Videocassette.

The Waverly Consort. 1992. *1492: A Portrait in Music.* Produced and directed by Eugene Enrico. 60 min. University of Oklahoma. Videocassette.

The World History Videodisc (non-European history): 2400 Images from Archives Around the World. 1991. Instructional Resources Corporation, Annapolis, MD. Videodisc. Phone: (800) 922-1711.

Simulations

Dahomey and the African Slave Trade. A simulation of the 1715 conference on the west coast of Africa. Write to Mark Williams, The Loomis Chaffee School, Windsor, CT 06095.

The Industrial Revolution: A Global Event. A simulation for Grades 9–12, written by Daniel Berman and Robert Rittner. Available: The National Center for History in the Schools, Department of History, University of California, Los Angeles, 5262 Bunche Hall, 405 Hilgard Ave., Los Angeles, CA 90095-1473. FAX: (310) 267-2103. For a description of all curriculum units available from NCHS, see this website: <www.sscnet .ucla.edu /nchs/>.

A Medieval Banquet in the Alhambra Palace. A simulation, edited by Audrey Shabbas, of Arab-Islamic Spain at its height and the siege of Granada. Available, along with slides of the Alhambra palace and music from the World of Islam, a tape cassette, from AWAIR: Arab World and Islamic

Resources and School Services, 2095 Rose Street, Suite 4, Berkeley, CA 94709.

People, Prices, and Products. A simulation game on early modern European social and economic structure. To purchase, send $19.95 and your address to "People, Prices, and Products," 68 Simsbury Road, West Granby, CT 06090.

The Pequot War. A documentary analysis of encounter in the New World. Included in Connecticut History on the Web, available online at <www.connhistory.org/>.

Water Wheels and Steam Engines, Parts I and II. Documentary material on the Industrial Revolution in Connecticut, with emphasis on industrialization in a small rural town, Samuel Colt, and Cheney Brothers Silk Manufacturers. Included in Connecticut History on the Web, available online at <www.connhistory.org/>.

World Music

Two noteworthy organizations offer extensive collections of world music with useful annotation:

The first is Smithsonian Folkways. See, for example, their compilation entitled *Wade in the Water*, compiled and annotated by Bernice Johnson Reagon, about the African and America concert spiritual tradition. For a catalogue, write: Smithsonian/Folkways Recordings, 955 L'Enfant Plaza, Suite 2600, Smithsonian Institution, Washington, DC 20560. Phone: (202) 287-3262.

Another organization is Ellipsis Arts. See, for example, *Voices of Forgotten Worlds: Traditional Music of Indigenous Peoples.* To learn more about the collections, write Ellipsis Arts, 20 Lumber Road, Roslyn, New York, NY 11576.

The Georgia Sea Islands songs referred to in Chapter 2 are from a compact disc, *Georgia Sea Island Songs*, available from New World Records, 701 Seventh Ave., New York, NY 10036. Phone: (212) 302-0460.

Two important video collections are indispensable for the incorporation of world music into the world history curriculum. They are:

The JVC Video Anthology of World Music and Dance. Produced by Ichikawa Katsumori. 30 vols. Victor Company of Japan, Ltd. 1994. In collaboration with Smithsonian/Folkways Recordings. Distributed by Rounder Records, Cambridge, MA 02140.

The JVC Smithsonian Folkways Video Anthology of Music and Dance of the Americas. Directed by Hiroaki Ohta. Victor Company of Japan, Ltd. 1995.

Distributed by Multicultural Media, 31 Hebert Road, Montpelier, VT 05602. Phone: (800) 550-9675.

World History on the Internet

One of the best, well-organized sites for exploring world history through primary sources is Paul Halsall's *Internet History Sourcebooks* at <www .fordham.edu/halsall>. Sourcebooks may be found on ancient history, medieval history, modern history, African, East Asian, Indian, Jewish, women's, global, and lesbian/gay/bisexual/transgender history. All sources may be printed and copied for educational use.

A somewhat comparable site for exploring world history through secondary sources is Hyperhistory Online at <www.hyperhistory.com>. This site contains colorful graphics, lifelines, time lines, maps, and a world history narrative covering 3,000 years. The time lines address the following topics: (1) science, technology, economy, discovery; (2) culture, philosophy, art, music, poetry; (3) religion, theology; (4) politics, war.

The World History Center, Northeastern University, and Its Affiliates

The World History Center at Northeastern
www.whc.neu.edu/

H-World, the electronic discussion list of the World History Association
http://h-net.msu.edu/~world

The New England Regional World History Association
www.whc.neu.edu/ner-wha

The World History Association and Its Affiliates
www.whc.neu.edu/wha/

The *Journal of World History* is the official journal of the World History Association, published twice a year. Individual subscriptions are $30.00 and include membership in the WHA. Send a check or money order to: Professor Richard Rosen, Executive Director, World History Association, Department of History and Politics, Drexel University, Philadelphia, PA 19104.

The *World History Bulletin*, also published twice a year, contains smaller scholarly articles and a section on the teaching of world history. It is sent only to members of the World History Association.

The World History Archives
    www.hartford-hwp.com /archives
    www.hartford-hwp.com /gateway/index.html

The Rocky Mountain World History Association
    www.woodrow.org/teachers/world-history/

Global Studies, Euro-Asian History, AP European History
    www.teleport.com /~arden /appage.htm

World Cultures
    www.wsu.edu:8080/~dee/ WORLD.HTM

Association of Asian Studies (especially the periodical *Education About Asia*)
    www.aasianstudies.org

AskAsia
    www.askasia.org

Images of World History
    www.mcad.edu /AICT/html /index.html

World History to 1500
    www.byuh.edu /coursework /hist201/

Women in World History
    www.womeninworldhistory.com

Africa Research Central
    http://africa-research.org

EuroDocs (primary historical documents from western Europe)
    http://library.byu.edu /~rdh /eurodocs/

Latin American History Resources
    http://lanic.utexas.edu /la/region /history/

The Yale Center for International and Area Studies
    www.yale.edu /ycias/